SCREW THE BITCH
DIVORCE TACTICS FOR MEN

© JEFF GAITHER 91

BY DICK HART

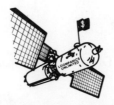

Loompanics Unlimited
Port Townsend, Washington

SCREW THE BITCH
  Divorce Tactics For Men

© 1991 by Dick Hart
Printed in USA

Published by:
Loompanics Unlimited
PO Box 1197
Port Townsend, WA 98368

Loompanics Unlimited is a Division of Loompanics Enterprises, Inc.

Cover by Jeff Gaither

ISBN 1-55950-069-7
Library of Congress
  Catalog Card Number 91-061587

Contents

1

There's No Such Thing as A "Nice" Divorce

This book is written by a man, for men, as a practical and tactical guide to handling divorce. It's a no-holds-barred discussion of defenses against being worked over and hung out to dry during a divorce. There's a real need for this book because many men are in need of "consciousness raising." Many men act as if they believe the feminist propaganda that "it's a man's world," and don't realize how badly the legal deck is stacked against them, in both marriage and divorce.

The women's liberation movement has caused restructuring of the laws, to gain "equal rights" for women. At the same time, it has carefully avoided demanding equal responsibility from women. The law often requires the husband to support his ex-wife, but no law obliges her to continue to cook for him or do his laundry. The result is that the law treats women as not just legally "equal," but specially privileged. This is why, in a divorce, it's the husband who usually gets it in the shorts.

This book is a practical manual for a married man who may be facing divorce. It lays out normal precautions, steps worth taking even when the relationship is rock-solid, because women certainly look out for their own interests inside and outside of marriage. We'll look at the history and role of marriage, and see how the relationship is often unequal, and loaded in the wife's favor.

The emphasis will be on self-protection, because the wife almost always has a hidden agenda, however much she may deny it and put on a smiling front. This agenda has two parts; self-interest and revenge.

The wife tries to obtain the best financial deal for herself. She may claim alimony by saying she's unable to work because she's been out of the job market for too long, or has to take care of several children. To gain sympathy from the court, she may claim that her husband mistreated her. She's actually out to skin the husband alive, both for her own benefit and to make life after divorce as hard on him as possible. In this case, if the husband "turns the other cheek," she'll use the other fist. Thus, a divorce can become very bitter, with both parties trying their best to hurt the other. This isn't limited to physical assault. In fact, physical assault is the rarest result of emotional violence in a divorce. There are other ways, and wives tend to be more vengeful than husbands. An important reason for this is the influence of their friends, as well as various cultural influences.

The wife may begin with a reasonable attitude, but may change her mind later. During discussions with her friends, she'll perhaps be influenced by a man-hater, who may convince her that the husband is a no-good male chauvinist pig, and deserves the worst. Unfortunately, there's a man-hater in every crowd. She may be a woman who's been through a painful divorce herself, and who has nothing good to say about men. This woman may also have a special vendetta against men, and preach a "take no prisoners" doctrine at every opportunity.

Another influence is rhetoric originating in the "women's rights" or "women's lib" movement, which preaches a man-hating doctrine of "make 'em pay." Under such influence, the wife may become very unreasonable, and try to hurt her husband as much as she can during the divorce proceedings.

We'll look at what can happen when things go wrong, and how it feels to have the roof fall in on you. We'll also look at the economic costs of correcting the situation. It's often hard to estimate, at the outset, how expensive a divorce can be. The rich can afford to spend millions. However, a wage-earner must consider the hidden costs, because an important part of survival is getting through divorce as cheaply as possible.

Those who have not been through a divorce can't fully appreciate the emotional turmoil and the pressure involved. The workload can be overwhelming, with too much to do in too little time. Your wife and her attorney may add to your problems, using legal harassment tactics. One separated husband, who had many assets his wife was trying to capture, put it very dramatically: "It's like being in the jungle, with a sniper out there, gunning for you."

Some find that the emotional stress makes it difficult to concentrate or think clearly, yet they must continue working at their regular employment, while simultaneously arranging the separation. Taking care of the details is a lot of work, and it may seem like holding down two or more jobs. Another hazard is that mistakes can be expensive, financially and emotionally.

Some people can't get through a divorce without some sort of "counseling," or more serious psychiatric help. One reason for this is the helpless feeling that results from facing a situation with which they can't cope. The feeling that life is going out of control can easily affect mental balance. Some people attempt suicide because of the stress, and some succeed.

The strain, unfortunately, is mainly on the husband. He has the responsibility, by custom and by law, of providing not only for himself, but for his wife and children. If he moves out, leaving his wife to live rent-free in the family house, he has to rent an apartment for himself. This leaves him paying for two households. He also faces an unequal contest, because his ex-wife can go to court to take as much of his income or assets as she can, especially if there are minor children to support. He often cannot hold back payments without hurting his children.

This book can help, because it's a guide to taking charge, and remaining in control, during both marriage and divorce. If you're involved in a bad marriage, there are practical steps you can take to protect yourself before the roof collapses. The earlier you begin, in fact, the more problems you can forestall.

How To Use This Book

This book is a nuts-and-bolts book, a guide to tactical divorce. It's not only a text, but also a workbook. The reason is that it's impossible to draw a road-map of the preparations for divorce, or a perfect plan to carry it through. Every person is different. Your wife may be reasonable or spiteful. Every situation is somewhat unlike others. You may feel that the best strategy is to appease your wife, or you may have decided that only a hard line is workable. This book can arm you with the essential knowledge, and lay out the basic procedures, but you have to make the plan yourself, to suit your own needs and your own schedule.

First, you need the right attitude. Do you let yourself be bull-dozed by women because you try to be a gentleman, instead of looking out for your own interests? Have you been convinced or cowed by the feminist propaganda that men always take un-fair advantage of women? Do you let your wife beat up on your self-esteem? Do you leave yourself open to wife-induced guilt, and are you willing to let your wife have anything she wants to relieve that guilt? If so, you need to stop seeing yourself as the bad guy, because if you become convinced that you're in the wrong, you'll have lost the most important part of the struggle.

Just think of it this way: If you're such a low-life bad guy, why did your spouse ever marry you? If you're a sleazeball, does that make your children sleazeballs too?

Start by seeing yourself as a decent and worthwhile person, no worse than your wife and probably a lot better, and you'll overcome the first obstacle to surviving divorce. You'll be better able to face the decisions, and handle the crushing workload.

Divorce survival involves a lot of details, and the logistics can be overwhelming. This book will show you how to spread the workload, so that you find the time to take care of important details. Forgetting an important detail is very easy when your life is in turmoil, and the checklists within these pages will serve as reminders during a trying time. Photocopy the lists to make working copies, using the margins for notes, and if you find it necessary to change the plan, just make another copy.

Although this book discusses divorce laws, it's not a substitute for an attorney's advice. Why not? First, the author is not an attorney. The more important reason, however, is that laws vary from state to state, both in wording and application. If your state is a "community property" state, the law regarding division of property will be different from the law in states which do not follow this principle. Another difference is the "no fault" divorce law. Many states, such as Arizona, California, Colorado, Florida, Hawaii, Iowa, and others, allow divorce simply on the grounds that the relationship isn't working, without requiring the plaintiff to prove that the spouse is guilty or deficient in any way. Other states with "no fault" laws are Kansas, Kentucky, Michigan, Minnesota, Missouri, Montana, Nebraska, Nevada,

North Carolina, Oregon, Washington, Wisconsin, Wyoming, and the District of Columbia.

The law constantly changes, because of legislation, and new interpretations of existing laws by courts. This is why any book dealing with the law starts becoming obsolete the moment it's finished.

Finally, we have to consider what really happens in court. Forget any notion of the court being an impartial arbiter making fair judgments based on "truth" and "justice." Any American court case, criminal or civil, is an "adversary proceeding," with each side trying to make the best possible presentation. It's more like a game, in which the goal is to pick up all the marbles. Often, what counts is not who's "right" or "wrong," but which side has the better attorney, or who can present his case better in front of a judge. As we'll see, attorneys often don't give it their best. Also remember that many divorces are settled "out of court."

This book does not make moral judgments. Some people feel that divorce is totally wrong. The Roman Catholic Church, for example, does not recognize divorce, any more than it recognizes a civil marriage. Some other religions take similar views.

There are also some limits in this book. Some people prefer "divorce Italian style," by killing their wives or having them killed. Others choose to use harassment or vandalism against spouses, for revenge, or to exert pressure. These tactics are outside the scope of this book.

There are also some problems you don't need a book to solve. If your wife takes the children and, regardless of the court's ruling, doesn't let you see them, you don't need a book to persuade you to carry out a "custodial" kidnaping.

As you go through these pages, you'll find a certain amount of repetition. The reason is that divorce has many facets, and they're all inter-related and interactive. One action affects several others, and it's important to tie them together, instead of dealing with each in isolation.

Surviving Tactical Divorce

Divorce is a fact of Twentieth Century American life. The odds of remaining married for life are ever-shrinking these days. Divorce is one drastic way out of an impossible situation. Yet, many men are reluctant to take this final step because of their uncertainty about the future. Lack of knowledge, and lack of preparation deters them from acting before the situation deteriorates further.

If it happens to you, don't cry over spilled milk. You'll need all your strength to survive the situation without becoming an emotional or financial wreck. The purpose of this book is to help you survive divorce, and survival means keeping control, instead of allowing the situation to run away with you.

Do yourself a big favor, if you're contemplating divorce. Go through this book thoroughly, scanning each page, to get a full understanding of what tactical divorce involves. You know your own wife and situation best. It's up to you to decide if you want to obtain a divorce, and to estimate how nasty it can get in your case.

As you read through this book, check out the source material. If you're like most men, you may have no idea of how vicious feminist ideology can be, and you may not believe it until you read some of these feminist articles and books yourself. Keep in mind that feminist writers have great influence upon many women, and that their man-hating philosophy is widespread. Act as if you believe it, and maybe you will avoid getting "Pearl Harbored" by an exploitative wife.

Therefore, keep in mind that divorce may become extremely nasty, through no fault of your own, if your wife takes the initiative and uses dirty tricks against you. Let's look at a few examples of what can happen in the next chapter. Remember that these have happened to real people, some of whom may be your friends.

2

Your Worst Nightmare

There are several possible nightmares for a man whose marriage falls apart. Although there are orderly ways of arranging separations, some wives go to extremes, driven by fear, revenge, or other motives. Let's look at a few possibilities:

■   You telephone home to find out if your wife wants you to pick up anything from the store on the way home from work. There's no answer. When you arrive, you find the apartment empty. You ask a neighbor if she knows where your wife has gone, and she tells you that she hasn't seen your wife since she left with the moving van.

What went wrong? You got "Pearl Harbored!"

■   The doorbell rings and a sheriff's deputy hands you a court order stating that you have half an hour to pack your personal items and move out. If you refuse, or try to enter your home again after you leave, you'll be thrown in jail. To pay for a hotel room for the night, you go to the bank, only to find that your wife's closed out your joint accounts, and that your credit cards are void. You're out on the street, confused, and with an uncertain future.

Again, you got surprised.

■ You'd seen the break-up coming, but didn't want to believe that the situation was hopeless. Today, when your wife tells you that she's leaving, you try to act like a "gentleman," and even smile as the moving van pulls away from your apartment with all the furniture. Later, the mail brings a bill from the credit card company, and you see that she's run your credit line to the limit on that card. The next week is hell for you, as you find several other bills in your mailbox, listing the charges your wife ran up on the credit cards before taking off. You can't pay the bills, because your wife has stripped your joint savings account down to ten dollars.

What went wrong in this situation? You weren't really surprised. You let the situation ride, perhaps hoping things would get better. Most importantly, you failed to keep control, and let the situation get away from you.

■ You and your wife have agreed to separate in what you think is an amicable fashion. After one discussion, she tells you tearfully that she'd feel better if you did not spend the night at home, and politely asks you to move out at once. Perhaps because you feel sorry for her, or perhaps because you're just a nice guy, you agree, and you pack a bag. You take a motel room, intending to obtain the rest of your clothing and your personal possessions after you find an apartment. Upon your return, you find the locks changed. Your wife tells you through the door that she threw your possessions into the garbage the day after you left.

Again, something went drastically wrong, and you could have avoided it. You underestimated your wife's hatred for you, and you failed to protect your assets.

It can get even worse if children are involved:

■ Your wife has gained custody of the children, and you have visitation rights. If you arrive late, she doesn't let you see them. If you arrive early, she tells you to wait in your car. At times, you arrive on time, and she won't open the door at all. If you return the children late, she hassles you. If you telephone your children, she hangs up the phone. She has you in court because you gave one of your children an air rifle. She again takes you to court because the house has no insulation, and for feeding your children "junk food," which she claims made them hyperactive. She takes you to court again, claiming that you're unfit to see your children because you have psychiatric problems. You're constantly being taken to court for additional payments, and your boss tells you that he might fire you if you keep losing time from work for court appearances.

What went wrong here? This is a case of not only marrying the wrong sort of person, but of failing to defend yourself adequately, even years after the ship hit the sand. However, it can get even worse:

■ Police officers come to your workplace to arrest you for molesting your own children. Your wife is the complainant, and you discover that she's simultaneously filing for divorce. You've been sandbagged, because you have to get bailed out of jail, and you've lost your job as a result of the arrest.

In the following pages, we're going to study ways to protect your financial and material assets, children, and legal rights as you move towards divorce. We'll see how you must plan ahead, to avoid taking on too much stress, or trying to do the impossible.

3

Manage Your Marriage

A favorable relationship helps avoid the need for divorce. It also makes it easier for you if the marriage deteriorates. To understand this, we have to take a quick look at marriage as an institution, and understand its history. The history of marriage provides insights into the way marriage is today, and the reasons for the changing roles of men and women in the relationship.

A Short History of Marriage

Marriage as we know it was originally set up as prescribed by various religions, and gradually came to legal status in the last few centuries. The original idea was a commitment for life, and this usually stood the test of time, until the Twentieth Century. Divorce was unknown, and marriage was for life. There were, however, provisions for annulment of the marriage, at least in the Roman Catholic Church. It was more important to have a substantial bribe for church authorities, than a good case, to obtain an annulment. This left ordinary people out of luck. There were, however, unofficial means of coping with the strains of a religious or civil marriage, even without dissolution.

Husbands had mistresses. Wives were also unfaithful, but there was an unfortunate double standard here. A husband who had sex outside of marriage was simply exercising masculine prerogative, but an unfaithful wife would have a hard time of it if discovered. The Old Testament records that adulteresses were stoned to death. Even with the advent of Christianity, which purportedly was a "kinder, gentler" religion, adulteresses were treated more harshly than adulterers. Today, Islamic fundamentalists prescribe stoning to death for women caught in adultery. This is an example of how, during most of history, women were treated as "chattel," or mere possessions.

The role of women in marriage gradually evolved. The idea of a partnership took hold, and in the last couple of centuries, the roles crystallized. The man was the breadwinner, as men before him had been hunters, and the woman took care of the home and children.

Women Gain Equality

Today, however, roles have almost reversed. Modern thought now regards subjugation of the wife as immoral, and there are laws protecting women's rights. The women's liberation movement has encouraged women to find jobs, to assure their economic independence.

In this country, both cultural factors and the economic situation have combined to help women's aspirations in the job market. People are materialistic, and they want the "good things" of life, such as cars, television sets, video recorders, etc.

It's also more difficult to raise a family on a single income. The result is that many married men today do not object if their wives work, whereas a couple of generations ago, it would have been almost unthinkable. A working wife was a stigma, and a reflection on the husband's ability to provide for his family.

Two generations ago, a working man could marry, buy a house, and raise several children on his pay alone. The entry of women into the job market resulted in lower pay for men, as a result of a "ripple effect." Today, employers find that they can employ women for the same work as men, in many fields. However, women do not get the same pay. This is true regardless of women's libbers, and regardless of the law. Here's how:

Full-time employees receive their paychecks and full benefit packages. Part-time employees, however, often receive lower hourly scale, and no benefits. Women entering the job market, either to supplement family income or to gain a sense of independence, increase the labor pool. This allows employers to have more part-timers on their staffs, also affecting full-time workers, most of whom are males. They now have to work for less, either in lower wages, or fewer hours. However, part-time workers are more likely to be women, because women often have to take care of families, as well as earn extra income. The net result is that women still work for less, and the promise of the libbers is still unfulfilled.

Reversing The Roles

The old adage; "You pay, you say; I pay, I say," influences the marital situation. When women were totally dependent upon their spouses for support, they had to be more submissive. Today, women are trying out their new economic and social equality, and some try to prove that they're more than equal. This has affected the divorce rate.

Marriage has always taken place at a fairly steady rate in this country. In 1895, for example, there were 8.9 marriages per 1,000 population. The rate hit a high point in 1945, with 12.2 marriages per 1,000 population, and gradually sunk to 10.2 per 1,000 in 1985, and 9.7 marriages per 1,000 people in 1988. Divorces, however, were rare in 1895, with only 0.6 per 1,000 population that year. By 1915, the rate had reached 1 divorce per 1,000 population, and 2 per 1,000 by 1940. In 1970, the rate had risen to 3.5 per 1,000, and by 1975, 4.8. The divorce rate peaked at 5.2 in 1980, then declined slightly to 5.0 in 1985 and 4.8 in 1988.[1]

The role of divorce has changed. Formerly, the double standard determined that a divorced woman was little better than a slut. Today, divorce is so common that this is a quaint and obsolete notion. In some circles, divorce is almost fashionable.

Women who earn their own incomes are much less dependent on husbands than those who do not. Tradition dictates, however, that alimony still exists. Alimony was a system of support payments based on the assumption that women had no independent means of support. This is no longer true, but alimony endures, and women's lib groups are not pushing very hard for its abolition.

The Community Property Scam

One concept we've seen enacted into law in some states is that of "community property." This states that assets acquired by either party during the marriage will be divided equally upon dissolution. At first, this appears to be fair, but actually, it's a fraud, because it ignores who earned the assets. The husband usually is the only wage-earner, or earns the higher income in two-income marriages.

Support Payments

Alimony is actually a form of punitive action against the husband, in the guise of support for a destitute wife. An emotional controversy, such as divorce, has undercurrents that some outsiders don't fully appreciate. A vengeful wife will want to make it as difficult as possible for her ex-husband to resume dating or remarry, and one way to do this is to cripple him financially, as a symbolic castration. The keys to doing this are the property settlement, alimony, and child support payments, if applicable.

One organization dedicated to obtaining maximum financial benefits for the woman is the "National Organization to Insure Survival Economics," which has an interesting acronym: "NOISE." This organization describes itself as a "one woman crusade to help the victims of divorce." The victims, of course, are women.

Many ex-wives expect alimony as a matter of course, and many judges will grant it, regardless of the ex-wife's ability to support herself. In a divorce action today, the material settlement is usually more important than the dissolution. Each side tries to get as much as possible. The wife wants a property settlement that leaves her well off, and the husband tries to avoid being financially crippled. It's what mathematicians call a "zero-sum game," because one side can gain only at the expense of the other. What one wins, the other loses.

This suggests that you ought to know if your wife has any savings or another source of income. Any money she has or earns will affect her standard of living, and if you can show that your wife is already earning part of the amount she needs, or claims to need, you'll be able to reduce your alimony payments. Likewise if she has inherited money, or is about to do so after the death of a relative. Keeping track of these factors can help your case.

Take this point very seriously. Many wives today have a nest egg, either savings or a source of income which they keep secret from their husbands. They can use it as "mad money," or as a survival kit.

Another aspect of divorce law which penalizes the man while favoring the woman is child support. The law states that the husband is responsible for supporting the children, and he must make payments dictated by the court until the children (usually in the wife's care) are grown. Even in states where the law does not specifically state that the husband must pay, it still works out that way. It almost never happens that an ex-wife must support either her ex-husband or the children.

One exception was Margaret Cheatham, who had married and supported a man who did not like to work, and after their divorce, paid him $125 per week until she found out that she didn't have to, under New York state law. This case is cited in *Womanlist*, which we'll discuss in depth below.

We see many statements that women lose out fearfully in divorce, and that men continue to move into higher income brackets while divorced women and their children descend into poverty. One book, written by a woman, uses statistical tables to demonstrate that families headed by females are often below the poverty level. The problem with these tables is that they include "families" consisting of women who had children out of wedlock, as well as divorcees.[2] Another source of confusion is that the figures include many ghetto residents who normally live below the poverty level, married or not.

Feminists who push these opinions neglect the plight of the widow, who is often worse off because there is no ex-husband to make support payments. Life insurance, if the husband carried it, is often inadequate, and part of it often pays funeral costs.

Social Security is often inadequate. The working widow faces the same handicaps as the working divorcee, and doesn't have the same economic advantages. Man-hating feminists aren't interested in this problem, because they can't stick it to a husband who's dead.

Women have always married as much for money as for love. A recent issue of *People* Magazine told of several young and pretty women who married wealthy older men. This may be only the appetizer for some, though.

Women interested in taking their ex-husbands to the cleaners can draw inspiration from cases cited in feminist publications, such as *Womanlist*.[3] The largest settlement recorded, between $10 million and $15 million, is that which Cristina Ford obtained from Henry Ford II in 1980.

"Bobo," Winthrop Rockefeller's ex-wife, got an award of $6,393,000 from him in 1954. Another woman, married five times, was Peggy Hopkins Joyce, who married men affluent enough to give her a total of $3,000,000 in divorce settlements.

It always pays to marry a man with money, as the ex-wife of Muhammad Ali showed when she divorced him. Khalilah Tobona won $2 million in the settlement. Tyrone Power was forced to give Linda Christian, his ex-wife, $1 million and a share of his present and future earnings when they split in 1955. This was despite Linda Christian's being a screen star in her own right, with an income many American women would have envied.

It seems that entertainers always get it in the shorts. Glen Campbell, well-known country and western singer, got taken to the cleaners, having to pay his ex-wife $500,000 as a starter. She also got 10,000 shares of stock in various companies, as well as shares of various other business interests he owned, and other miscellaneous benefits.

Being an intellectual, even a Nobel-prize winning author, doesn't help. Saul Bellow, who won the Nobel Prize for literature in 1976, had to give his ex-wife, Susan Glassman Bellow, a lump-sum alimony payment of $500,000. Next, she was awarded $800 per month child-support payments. Bellow also had to pay her lawyers, and this came to another $200,000.

It's hard to understand what these women could have done, or suffered, to earn such huge sums. People injured or killed in traffic accidents usually get far less, even counting today's stupendous medical bills.

Some women like to think that, without them, their husbands wouldn't be where they are today. In fact, few women share their husbands' work; far fewer than years ago, when "mom and pop" businesses were common.

There are exceptions, however. A few women work to put their husbands through school. In this regard, the husband has received a very tangible benefit from the wife, and California's "Sullivan vs. Sullivan" case and the legislation that accompanied it set guidelines for repaying the wife for what she put into the marriage. It's important to stress that cases in which the wife supports the husband while he studies are exceptional, not typical.

In today's real world, the husband normally goes off to work, while the wife either remains at home or goes off to her own employment. Many married couples with children feel they need two incomes, and they put children into day care facilities while they work.

At times, marriage can have a negative effect on the husband's earning power. In certain instances the emotional strain of a deteriorating marriage impairs the husband's ability to work at top efficiency. In other cases, wives hold their husbands back. Executive recruiters typically want to interview the wife, as well as the husband, because they want to appraise whether the wife will be a help or a hindrance to her husband in his work, which may require long hours or extensive travel. Some executive candidates don't get hired because of their wives. The recruiter may be impressed by the husband's talents, but finds that the wife lacks class, or is too introverted to take part in the social life which is part of the executive scene.

Another characteristic of divorce books written by women is that they tend to dismiss the father's rights, and consider fathers' complaints of unfair treatment as unjustified. They ignore the blatant unfairness of laws that automatically award custody of children to the mothers. They deny that men "get taken to the cleaners," or that fathers are ever denied access to their children by the mother.[4]

Another claim of feminist rhetoric is that, despite recent reforms in divorce laws, the woman is still getting a bad deal. Despite "community property," which awards the wife a stake in everything the husband earned during the marriage, it's still not enough. They complain that the divorce settlement does not include "educational achievements, earning abilities, or career development."[5] The implications of this are frightening. Even 100% isn't enough, as these feminists want a share in the husband's earnings for the rest of his life.

Some resent the economic settlement, even though it leaves them the family house, while the husband goes to live in a small apartment. Their expectations appear to be that life should go on as before, with the husband paying all of their bills, without regard to his own needs. The parent with children allegedly needs 80% of the previous family income to maintain the same standard of living.[6] This doesn't leave the husband much for himself.

The actual amount of money involved doesn't appear to appease the tastes of some divorcees. One pampered woman complained that she "barely got by" on a budget of $2,000 per month. This left her unable to afford to pay a cleaning woman and gardener.[7]

This is typical of the radical view that some women have found attractive. They feel that marriage to a man for a few years gives them the right to everything he has, and a choke-hold on his earning power for the rest of his life. Some even demand a share of the husband's retirement income. The Social Security Act will pay benefits to an ex-wife, if the marriage lasted for ten years.

Despite large settlements, and an increasing array of methods for stripping a man's assets, some people still push the viewpoint that women inevitably get the worst of it in a divorce. One female author states that women "are suffering the brutality of divorce at an unprecedented rate."[8] This viewpoint ignores men's suffering.

The combination of greedy women, and divorce lawyers with the mentality of killer sharks, results in an all-out effort to strip the husband of as many assets as possible. In this regard, the lawyer who charges $175 per hour is not going to be interested in a case involving a husband who earns only slightly above minimum wage. If there's money to be had, though, he'll go after it, often charging the wife up-front for his services.

Any man with more assets than a migrant worker should be careful whom he marries, and take precautions to ensure that he doesn't get skinned alive if he and his wife split. One way is with a pre-nuptial agreement.

Pre-nuptial Agreements

Obviously, the best way to handle a divorce is never to have one. However, in many parts of the country, each year brings more divorces than marriages. American family life has become very unstable, and divorce today is an everyday fact. Still, while a marriage lasts, it's in your interest to keep it stable. If it begins to fail, maintaining stability will help you to control the situation.

One way of keeping it stable and avoiding unpleasant surprises is using a pre-nuptial agreement, a document that lays out each person's role and financial interest. It's especially valuable when rich marries poor.

Some people pretend love when they're only interested in the good life a wealthy mate can offer them. A female who does this is a whore or gold-digger. Males also play this game, and there are gigolos who prey on older or ugly women who have the means to maintain them in style. A written agreement that, in case of a split, each partner comes out of it with the assets he or she put in, will forestall some of these marriages. It will also put the damper on an ambitious wife, as she will have less incentive to break up the marriage if she knows that she can't strip the husband bare.

It's not too surprising that a woman might not like a pre-nuptial agreement. One woman who expressed herself in print on this subject is Erma Bombeck, a satirist who sometimes discusses serious topics, in her March 8, 1990 column. Her verdict is that a pre-nuptial agreement's only effect is to "set you up for failure." She blames the richer partner for "insecurity," and identifies this partner by the masculine pronoun, thereby making her position clear. Apparently, she feels that a man should believe unquestioningly that his prospective bride wants him only for his good looks and charm, even though he may be wealthy and she may be penniless, cheerfully leaving himself wide open for economic rape if the marriage fails.

We've already seen how the feminist viewpoint sees large divorce settlements, and presents the female beneficiaries as idols for others to follow. This makes it obvious that a man who has assets to protect should be doubly careful when contemplating marriage. If your assets are worth protecting with large insurance policies, burglar alarms, and other means, you should not hesitate to employ a pre-nuptial agreement to avoid getting cleaned out by a gold-digger. Remember, if you don't take the initiative to protect yourself, you're losing.

Keeping Information to Yourself

Don't let your wife know all about your business. Never let her know how much money you've really got. If she insists upon knowing, maybe you've married the wrong sort of gal.

Of course, you may feel that, as a matter of fair play, marriage partners should have no secrets from each other. This is perfectly true. The problem is that most marriage partners aren't perfect people.

There are specific types of damaging information you need to keep under cover:

Financial

Keep your wife guessing about your income, and how you spend it. The best system is to give her a household allowance, and keep the rest out of her sight and reach. This simple precaution prevents her from making an estimate of what sort of alimony payments she might expect in case she's contemplating divorce.

Another aspect of financial discretion has to do with taxes. You may have hidden income, and the best reason not to let your wife know about it is that she may use this information against you in case of a split. Although a wife may not testify against her husband in court, in certain types of cases, anything to do with taxes is an important exception. Your wife need not actually testify. She need only contact the Internal Revenue Service, in a fit of pique, and point the finger. They'll do the rest.

If, for example, you've let it slip that you're diverting some cash income into a safe deposit box, instead of reporting it, she may let her fingers do the walking and dial the IRS. If she can give them the box number, and perhaps even a copy of your key, they'll have most of their work done for them. Likewise, if she knows you have bank accounts under aliases, complete with alternate Social Security numbers, she can blow the whistle if she gets mad at you. This is why you should be very discreet if you use a safe deposit box for special purposes. Don't even list it as a deduction on your income-tax return, where she and IRS agents can see it.

Always keep in mind that an informer for the IRS also has a financial interest. Although IRS Agents keep their "Turn in a Friend" program low-key, they do offer up to ten percent of tax money recovered as a reward. Your estranged wife, therefore, can earn a few extra bucks, as well as get revenge, by shafting you.

Guilty Secrets

We assume that you're a straight arrow, but we also have to keep in mind the occasional reader who may have an unusual taste. If you have any vices, don't advertise them. If, for example, you live in a state listing adultery as grounds for divorce, getting a little "action" on the side may be very expensive. The judge will punish you for it by increasing your support payments. We've already seen how your wife can cause you problems with the IRS, which makes it important that you don't allow her access to any evidence she can turn over to the police.

In case you don't fully appreciate how your wife can do a number on you in a criminal matter, let's quickly go over how police officers develop evidence in criminal cases. Typically, information from a snitch provides their first lead. With that, they petition a court for a search warrant to seek out specific evidence. A search warrant is a court order allowing police investigators to search your home, office, car, etc., without your permission, for evidence pertaining to the crime which they're investigating. It limits police authority to search, in very specific ways. If, for example, they're investigating stolen televisions, they can only search areas large enough to accommodate TV sets, although a gray area may allow them to search desk drawers for information regarding the thefts. If they find illegal drugs, however, these are excluded from the search, and can't be introduced in evidence.

The search warrant affidavit must deal with "probable cause," showing good reason for a search of specific premises. The "exclusion rule" formulated by the U. S. Supreme Court states that illegally obtained evidence cannot be used in a prosecution.

If your wife decides to blow the whistle on you, she can invite police investigators to search the premises. With her permission, they're home free. They can search for as long as she allows, and wherever she allows. If they find stolen TV sets, fine; they can use them in evidence. If they find kiddy porn, that's fine, too: more evidence to use against you. If they find illegal drugs, they've got you, and they won't let go.

Some vices aren't very serious, or even illegal. The police can't nail you for them, but they can still work against you, if your wife knows how to use them. If you drink heavily, but can keep it from affecting your work, you're not in terribly bad shape, even though it's hard to keep a wife from knowing about a drinking habit. Always keep in mind, though, that she may turn on you if ever you're seeking another job with a firm that has a bias against drinkers. Some employers actually conduct background checks, and this can include interviewing an ex-wife. This is especially true if you're applying for a government job, or a private industry position that requires a security clearance.

Government security investigators look for traits such as heavy drinking, gambling, and other activities that are not illegal in themselves, but may make you a security risk.

If you "do" recreational drugs, you should be aware that some employers won't hire anyone who uses illegal drugs, even during off-duty hours. Today, more employers are requiring urine tests of their applicants. A malicious ex-wife can "put the mouth" on you if you're applying for employment at one of these companies and their investigator contacts her. Even if you pass their urine test, they'll just assume that you're abstaining temporarily to avoiding failing the test.

The real kiss of death is an emotionally charged illegal act or hobby. For argument's sake, let's assume that you're into "kiddy porn," collecting pictures of naked little girls or boys. A few of these photos, left anywhere your wife may find them, can sink your marriage, but that's only the good news. If she calls the cops and spills her guts, you'll have a king-size problem around your neck.

Likewise, if you're working in a sensitive occupation, and selling secrets to the Soviets. Remember what happened to the Walker spy ring. John Walker spent almost his entire U. S. Navy career selling information on top-secret codes and cryptographic machines to the Soviet espionage service. He got away with it during his entire career, recruiting both other navy personnel and his son to supply him with material to pass to the Russians. After retiring from the navy, he kept running his spy ring, while the FBI and other security forces remained unaware. What finally sunk Walker was that his estranged wife turned him in!

The other ramification regarding sensitive secrets is blackmail, with which we'll deal when we get to negotiating the settlement.

Discretion

Be discreet. Learn to keep your mouth shut. Remember, information is always a potential weapon. Also remember that your wife may be trying to find out damaging information about you. Certain people, whom you might have accepted as friends, might actually be trying to "pump" you for information your wife can use against you. Other people whom you trust might be prompted by jealousy or other motives to repeat what you say to your wife.

There are two parts to maintaining discretion; need-to-know, and revealing feelings, not facts.

"Need-to-know" is the basic principle. Don't tell anyone anything crucial unless they need to know it, to help you. You may have to reveal certain facts to your lawyer or accountant, for example, but not to your drinking buddy.

The second point is that you may feel the need to talk to someone, to vent your emotions. Reveal feelings, not facts. You might say that you're worried about how your wife will take care of the children in your absence, but never reveal, for example, that you're hiding two thousand dollars in a safe deposit box.

Wives From Hell

There are several types of wives who cause unstable relationships, because of their beliefs, orientations, or lifestyles. Marrying any of these gives you a less-than-even chance of remaining married. Let's check off several types to avoid like the plague.

The Women's Libber

The libber is very concerned about women's "rights," but always at the expense of men. She won't, however, discuss the responsibilities that normally go with rights. The special pleading for "equality" often means wanting to be more than equal. The reasons for this are not surprising.

Those who saw the public television documentary on gay life in America know how the "women's liberation" movement began among a clique of lesbians. Some spin-offs from the movement were very outlandish, and revealing. One short-lived organization in New York City named itself "S.C.U.M." or the "Society For Cutting Up Men."[9] This type of women's libber won't give a man an even break; she'll try to break his balls, instead.

Another example was the women's columnist who sneeringly remarked upon the introduction of large-size condoms, such as Maxx, and Magnum, for men who are above average in penis size. She saw this as an expression of ego-tripping by some men, even though women have for decades had brassieres with varying cup sizes. Women who wear D cups, for example, because of their large breasts, are apparently acceptable.

With this mentality, it's not surprising that a women's libber puts so much strain on the relationship that it soon becomes intolerable. She'll take credit for everything that goes well, and blame her husband for everything that doesn't. If she doesn't get her way, she blames the man, and looks to the law to exact revenge. It's always no-win for the husband.

The "Assertive" Game-player

This type is closely related to the libber, and often is one. She believes that she has to be "assertive" in any situation or relationship, to avoid being dominated. Assertiveness becomes an end in itself, instead of a means to an end. It's easy to recognize the type, because their behavior is very conspicuous.

One example is the woman who is to meet a friend at an airport, but misses her at the gate because she wasn't looking carefully. She goes over to the ticket counter, plants herself ahead of other people in line, and demands to know if her friend's name was on the passenger list. She informs the clerk that she's not moving until she finds out what happened to her friend. If you make the mistake of getting into a relationship with this type, don't be surprised if she steamrollers you, too.

Another example is the woman who constantly interrupts, to the point of interjecting herself into a conversation between two other people. This is more than rude manners; it's outright pushiness. You can see this when you ask a third person a question, and she butts in to provide the answer herself. She appears determined to push her viewpoint onto you, even though you hadn't asked her.

The Loser

Losers exist among both sexes. These are people with histories of repeated marriages and divorces. Some accumulate a dozen or more. No doubt, a psychologist might produce a theory regarding why some people keep getting married, although all of their relationships fall apart, but for our purposes, it's enough to point out that marrying such a person is asking for trouble.

The Drifter

Some people like nomadic lifestyles, never remaining in one place, or job, for as long as a year. They also prefer changing partners. Such people can be very interesting, and even exciting to know, but they don't keep stable relationships. If you marry one, you'll find that nothing you can do will keep her happy. Sooner or later, she'll find fault with you, as she's found fault with every job she's ever had, every place she's ever lived, etc. In the end, she'll leave you for greener pastures.

Protecting Yourself

The simplest way to avoid getting into a relationship with the wrong person is to keep your eyes and ears open, and to use your common sense. It helps a lot if you're a good listener, instead of a non-stop talker, because people will tell you the most amazing things about themselves if you just listen.

You can often hear danger signals. The woman who tells you how she ripped off her previous husband is one to treat politely, but not to take seriously. So is the type who tells you about the expensive presents and expensive vacations provided by a previous boyfriend or husband. It's obvious that her interests are purely materialistic, and that she's simply a legalized prostitute.

Another topic for alert is any theme that has man-hating in the background. The topic may be rape, but if the speaker shows strong emotion about it, it suggests that she may have been raped herself, and may be holding a grudge against men. As long as you're not the rapist, it's not your problem, and you must not let her make it your problem.

When there are other people present, it pays to remain in the background, to watch and listen to how she interacts with others, both male and female. The reason is that you may not be able to make an objective evaluation if you're personally involved. You may not be sure if the problem lies with her, or with you.

Does she make strongly derogatory comments about a person when they're not around, then greet him or her with a broad smile and very warm manner? Does she appear to love to argue, picking arguments with others over minor points? What are her favorite conversational topics? These can point to a problem. Look, listen, and think.

The Wife Loses, Too

With today's charged atmosphere, many women see divorce only as a way of taking their husbands to the cleaners, and don't realize the impact it will have upon their lifestyles. An obvious one is financial, but many aspects aren't immediately visible. The woman who believes the feminist propaganda may not realize that there is only one pie to divide, and that all of the slices together will never add up to more than 100%.

One very serious problem today is health insurance. After the divorce, you may drop your ex-wife from your coverage, unless she has a very sharp attorney who has succeeded in persuading the court to make this part of the settlement. If you're under a group health plan at work, she'll have to find individual coverage, which is much more expensive. If she has a pre-existing condition, she'll find it very rough.

If there's only one family car, in your name, it's almost certain you'll get to keep it. After all, you need it to commute to work. Without you to take her shopping, or to the doctor, etc., she'll find life a bit more difficult.

She may get a car of her own, or may already have a car, if you've been a two-car family. However, she won't get the second-car discount. This will increase her costs.

Establishing credit will be difficult for her, unless she's been employed while you were married. A wife accustomed to credit-card living will be seriously inconvenienced.

Meeting another man may be difficult, depending on her age, looks, personality, and whether or not she has children. Many men lose interest very quickly once they find out a prospective date has a child or two from a former marriage. This is one factor, however, that can kick right back at you. If you're paying alimony and child support, the best thing that can happen to you is for her to re-marry. With another spouse supporting her, your financial liability will drop sharply, or vanish altogether. An ex-wife who remains unmarried can be on your back for many years.

Sources

1. National Center For Health Statistics, U. S. Department of Health and Human Services.

2. *Mothers and Divorce*, Terry Arendell, Berkeley, CA, University of California Press, 1989, pp. 1-3. The tables are taken from U. S. Census Bureau figures, and are on Pages 172 and 173. These tables show family status and poverty, but only list "female-headed families," without distinguishing between those who are divorced and those who were never married. It's easy to paint a misleading picture with statistics such as these, because they include females of minority and lower socio-economic groups who never worked, and whose principal occupation appears to be perpetuating welfare families.

   One author who treats this topic with more honesty is Mary Ann Mason, who points out in *The Equality Trap* that "many are the result of unwed mothers." (p. 235.)

3. *Womanlist*, Marjorie Weiser and Jean S. Arbeiter, New York, Atheneum, 1981, pp. 269-270.

   Newspaper columns also reinforce the greedy and exploitative viewpoint. One woman, whose letter was published in Ann Landers' column on May 26, 1990, described how she profited during a divorce from an unfaithful husband. Her husband was very well off and she "showed him no mercy." She felt that he deserved to "have his clock cleaned," and she proposed that wives "take every dime they can get." This is one of the most explicit confessions of raw, naked greed in print, and is worth looking up and reading to understand why husbands get taken to the cleaners. Landers endorsed this viewpoint, adding her weight to encourage wives to savage their husbands when they can.

4. *Mothers and Divorce*, p. 6. This book cites the statements of fathers' groups, and treats them as "myths," and "assumptions." This author also mentions examples of difficulties divorcing women have had with lawyers (pp. 10-14), such as failure to return phone calls, and failure to keep their clients informed, as if incompetent lawyers have only female clients.

   Mary Ann Mason (*Equality Trap*) regards "no-fault" divorce and the community property split as inherently unfair to the ex-wife, because dividing the married couple's assets usually requires that the family house be sold (p. 53). Apparently, she feels that the wife should get the majority of the assets.

5. *Ibid.*, p. 29.

6. *Making Fathers Pay: The Enforcement of Child Support*, David Chambers, Chicago, IL, University of Chicago Press, 1979.

7. *Mothers and Divorce*, p. 45.

8. *The Equality Trap*, Mary Ann Mason, Simon and Schuster, 1988, p. 19.

9. *Ibid.*, Page 40. In many ways, Mary Ann Mason's book is the most intelligently written of the books by women cited here. Mason takes the viewpoint that many of the laws granting women "equality" were passed with the approval and support of women's organizations, and that these laws had unforeseen after-effects in lessening the husband's responsibility to the marital relationship. She also proposes certain sensible changes in laws covering support payments, such as allowing them as deductions.

4

Early Warning Signals

It's in your best interest to avoid being surprised in a marital break-up. There's no absolute way to avoid being surprised, but if you're reasonably alert, you can catch some of the early danger signs. This section outlines how to acquire information you need to keep control of the situation. It also lists sources of information, both overt and covert, and describes how best to use them.

Alertness

This is the basic principle. It's also the one easiest to ignore, either from laziness, or trust and good nature.

It's nice to feel that you can trust your wife, and it's true that trust is one of the basic building-blocks of an intimate relationship. It's also true that love is blind, and that you can get into a mental state wherein you ignore what would be obvious to anyone else.

Watchfulness doesn't mean adopting an unnaturally suspicious attitude. It doesn't mean becoming paranoid. If you're extremely insecure, you shouldn't be married to anyone. You must, however, be aware of what's obvious, because often there are obvious signs that something is terribly wrong.

You're unlikely to hear the back door slam seconds after you come home, and see a partly-dressed man running down the street and find half his clothes on your bed. That happens mainly in movie comedies. More likely, you're going to see something less startling, a detail you weren't meant to see, and this will probably happen by accident. It may also happen through carelessness, because people make mistakes. Finally, you may notice certain details, including changes in behavior, that are impossible to hide.

You might notice her buying new clothes, including sexy underwear, and having her hair done more often. Ask yourself: "Is this all for me?" Wait and see, and keep your eyes open.

You also may find her going to more club meetings with "the girls," and even joining a bowling league.

It's worth repeating: Be alert and watchful. Even if you think you're a bit paranoid, remember that paranoids have enemies too.

Watching the Mail

If you're home to receive the mail when it arrives, it's always a good idea to look at return addresses on anything addressed to your wife. There are two reasons for this: to observe the pattern, and to note anything that deviates from the pattern.

Most mail is uninteresting. Magazines, book club subscriptions, and the many pieces of advertising that comprise "junk mail" are hardly worth a second look. However, there are certain types of mail worth scrutinizing very carefully.

Mail From A Bank

Anything from a bank or other financial institution is worth investigation, especially if it's addressed to your wife alone. Does your wife maintain a secret account? This is often a tip-off that something is not right. If you find that your wife has maintained a separate account or two since before your marriage, you may suspect that she's not fully committed to the marriage. This is especially true if she hasn't told you. If you've had only joint accounts, and you become aware that she's recently opened a separate account, that's a danger signal. This is especially true if the account is in a different city.

An Attorney's Return Address

This is a possible cause for concern. While anyone about to file for divorce should be discreet, to avoid informing the partner until it's convenient, some people are stupid or careless, and tip off the partner by sending critical material through the mail.

Mail To Another Address

This is a definite alert signal. You normally won't see this, but your wife may carelessly leave an envelope laying where you do spot it. It's important to check it out as soon as possible. If it's addressed to her "care of" a friend of hers at another address, you can be sure that she's doing something she doesn't want you to know about. If the address is unfamiliar, go there yourself to see what you can. The odds are that it'll be within reach, because she has to pick the mail up herself. Look for a mail drop, such as one of the "Mail Box," or "Mail 'N More" franchises.

Absences

Absences, both explained and unexplained, may be cause for concern. They may signal that your wife is having an affair, or that she's looking for another place to live. Either way, find out.

You don't have to be heavy-handed about this. Discretion is vital, especially when you have only a suspicion, not proof. If your wife tells you that she'll be spending each Wednesday night attending classes at the local junior college, check the mileage on the car, just to be sure.

Telephone Calls

These may signal something important. This goes beyond wondering about a male caller. Most of these are salesmen, anyway, and many of them will pretend to be personal friends in order to get through.

Telemarketing tactics aside, you ought to be watchful if your wife makes long telephone calls. They may just be gossip with a friend, or they may signal something more serious. Be aware that you can listen in or record conversations, and it may be worth the effort.

It also may happen that a representative from an apartment or real estate management office, or a moving company, calls for your wife. In such a case, always ask for the company name, and a number so that she may return the call. Follow up intensively on this. You may not have much time.

Income Tax Returns

Always scrutinize these carefully. If you make your returns out yourself, look carefully at every piece of paper your wife gives you, instead of just jotting down the relevant figures. A federal tax return requires listing all sources of income, and you may find a Form 1099 listing interest from a bank account you never knew she had. Likewise, a stockbroker may furnish a Form 1099 listing dividends on stocks of which you were unaware.

But what if your wife doesn't hand you the Form 1099 she receives? What then?

In theory, every stockbroker, every bank, and every company that pays fees, dividends, or interest sends a copy of each Form 1099 to the IRS. In theory, IRS agents cross-check these with income sources listed on each tax return, to verify the correctness of the amounts declared. In practice, the IRS is so inefficient that only 25%, at most, of Form 1099s are cross-checked. The rest go into shredders or incinerators. However, this still leaves a 1 in 4 chance that, if your wife has a source of income she's trying to keep from you, the IRS will catch up with her. If she does not declare the income, an agent may discover it, by comparing copies of Form 1099 with the tax return, find the discrepancy and call you in for an audit. At that time, the moment of truth, you'll find out what she's been concealing from you.

Another item to watch is a deduction for a safe deposit box. This is a trick IRS investigators use when seeking out hidden assets. If your wife has a safe deposit box she's hidden from you, she may forget herself and list it as a deduction. There's no way you can get into it without her permission, but at least you'll know it's there, and will be able to draw the proper conclusions.

Another cause for suspicion is filing of separate returns. Federal tax laws give married couples a break for joint filing, and if your wife insists on filing separately, there may be something seriously wrong. If she refuses to let you see her tax return, you know beyond doubt that it's "Condition Red."

5

Dirty Tricks
Wives Use

Your wife may be ahead of you in planning for divorce. As we've seen, she may be setting money aside, consulting an attorney, and making other preparations to dump you. Wives also use other techniques that, because of their deviousness, belong in the "dirty tricks" department.

Denying Sex

One of the worst hypocrisies in the way law and custom view marriage is that the husband's "infidelity" is a sin or crime. Perhaps this is a reaction to the harsh treatment of unfaithful wives described in some religious writings, but today the pendulum has swung too far the other way.

Some wives will deny sex to their husbands as a pressure tactic, to force concessions in the relationship. Although many marriage counselors agree that denying sex is dirty fighting, some wives still use this tactic. Withholding sex for a fur coat, for example, is a blatant example of the legalized prostitution some marriages have become.

The truly nasty, calculating wife withholds sex as a prelude to divorce, secretly hoping to provoke her husband into an affair which she can use against him in court. This tactic is fading, as more states adopt "no fault" divorce laws.

Defense against this is simple. If your wife begins to withhold sex, go for a divorce ASAP. This is more than an early warning sign; it means she's begun to work seriously against you, and if you stick to the relationship in the hope that things will get better, you're going to lose.

Be especially careful if you live in one of the few states that still allows adultery as grounds for divorce. These are, at the time of writing: Alabama, Alaska, Arkansas, Connecticut, Delaware, Georgia, Idaho, Illinois, Louisiana, Maine, Maryland, Massachusetts, New Hampshire, New Jersey, New Mexico, New York, North Dakota, Ohio, Oklahoma, Pennsylvania, Rhode Island, South Carolina, South Dakota, Tennessee, Texas, Utah, Vermont, Virginia, West Virginia, and Puerto Rico. If your wife holds out on you, you can be sure that she's setting you up for an adultery charge. Moreover, in some states, adultery is still in the penal code, and you may be letting yourself in for criminal prosecution. Of course, public prosecutors rarely pursue this type of case, because they've got a tremendous volume of more serious crimes needing attention, but a malicious wife and her aggressive lawyer can light enough fires to get you charged.

Provoking Violence

Another tactic is provoking the husband to violence. This is an almost fool-proof tactic for the wife to try, because it often works and the danger is minimal. Very few instances of domestic violence end with death. Most husbands who become violent with their wives are immediately remorseful, and the wives take advantage of the guilt induced by the incident.

One way wives provoke husbands is to be completely unreasonable during an argument, to frustrate the husband and make him lose his temper. If he gets violent, she's got him.

This is a very dangerous situation for the husband because it can work against him in more than one way. First, cruelty is grounds for divorce in about as many states as adultery. A few, however, specify "physical" cruelty, such as striking the wife.

The second reason is the trendy "domestic violence" issue. Your wife can have you arrested for violence. If you spend a few days in jail, you can lose your job, as well. As we'll see, your wife can even have you locked out of your home by convincing a judge that she's "afraid" of you.

Finally, domestic violence inevitably influences child custody and visitation rights. If your wife can show some cuts and bruises to a judge, and convince him that you're a brute, she can keep you from your children.

You can forestall this, but only if you're really honest with yourself. First, can you control your temper? Can you restrain yourself when your wife becomes so obnoxious that you get an urge to slam her head into the wall? If you have any doubts about this, you'd better take some special precautions.

Never be afraid to walk out of an argument. When you see that your wife's being especially nasty and provocative, leave the room before the emotional level of the argument gets too high. Ignore her taunts. Just leave, and return when you and she have cooled off enough to forestall violence.

Be especially wary if you drink alcohol. Wives study their husband's habits for weaknesses or anything they can use against them. If you've had a before-dinner drink, and your wife begins an argument, watch out! She might be trying to set you up. Remember, if you strike her, and she calls the cops, alcohol on your breath will count very heavily against you. In fact, you won't have a chance. Unlike the laws dealing with drunk driving, there's no requirement for a breath or blood alcohol test in domestic violence cases. It won't matter if your Blood Alcohol Level is .01%, or .001%. Your wife's statement that you struck her in a drunken rage, combined with the police report that you had alcohol on your breath, will sink you in court.

If you're facing this situation, give up drinking for the duration. This means even "social" drinking, because of the possibility of your wife's friends testifying against you one day. Remember that sworn testimony can be "slanted" to give the impression the witness or attorney wants. Imagine yourself in court one day, listening to one of your wife's friends saying: "Charlie had a drink or two every time they came to the house." Imagine several of her friends in a row, delivering similar testimony, and building up a picture of constant and uncontrollable drinking.

Avoid arguments in public. Obviously, your wife would have a case against you if you were to threaten or strike her in front of witnesses. Therefore, don't even argue with her in front of other people, especially if you know that they're on her side. Anything you say will be used against you.

A simple way to handle the problem, if your wife gets nasty and contentious with you in front of others, is to reply: "We can talk about this later." Don't raise your voice, and don't try to answer directly any insulting statements she might make. Don't display any signs of irritation or temper, because that, too, can be used against you. Just back off, so that there can be no doubt regarding who is the aggressor.

The final problem comes with the outright frame-up. Just as some women will muss their hair and tear their clothes to support a fabricated charge of rape, some frame their husbands for domestic violence. If you see it coming, the best plan is to leave at once. Move out, or even run away, but leave.

Desertion

One of the clearest examples of the way the laws are stacked against the husband is that 31 states still list "desertion" as grounds for divorce. This means that you're damned if you do, and damned if you don't, leaving the door wide open for the wife to put her husband into a "no win" situation.

Relentless verbal harassment can provoke you to violence. You may, instead, decide that you don't need the hassle, and leave home. If you do, you may leave yourself vulnerable to a charge of desertion, which is grounds for divorce in states that still recognize this.

The news isn't all bad, though. Many states specify a period of time, ranging from 6 months in West Virginia to 7 years in Vermont. This prevents frivolous charges of desertion by a spiteful wife against a husband who simply went to visit relatives for a few days. What it means for you, though, is that you have a time cushion in which to get a divorce going. Best of all, get the divorce going before you move out. The ideal situation is to meet the process server as you're walking out for the last time.

Dirty Tricks Galore

There is an array of dirty tricks wives and ex-wives use against their mates, such as false charges of child abuse, impeding visitations, and false claims of non-support. We'll cover these in the appropriate chapters.

Vital Information

Preparing well ahead of time provides you with a head start if a crisis comes. You'll have made the basic decisions, and you'll merely be following through on your ground-work.

The reason that this is important is that going through a divorce is hard work. Think about the last time you moved, and the physical work that went with it. Divorce is like that, but more complicated.

One way to reduce the confusion of the last-minute scramble is to gather the information you'll need ahead of time, and to keep it up to date. Let's begin by listing financial information. Photocopy the following pages, filling in the blanks as appropriate. As the situation changes, make another photocopy, filling in the corrections.

Bank Accounts

1. _____
   (Bank Name)   (Address)

   _____
   (Phone Number)   (Checking Acct #)   (Savings Acct #)

2. _____
   (Bank Name)   (Address)

   _____
   (Phone Number)   (Checking Acct #)   (Savings Acct #)

3. _____
   (Bank Name)   (Address)

   _____
   (Phone Number)   (Checking Acct #)   (Savings Acct #)

4. _____
   (Bank Name)   (Address)

   _____
   (Phone Number)   (Checking Acct #)   (Savings Acct #)

Credit Cards

(Bank/VISA)	(Account #)	(Phone Number)
(Bank/MasterCard)	(Account #)	(Phone Number)
(Bank/Am. Express)	(Account #)	(Phone Number)
(Bank/Other)	(Account #)	(Phone Number)
(Gasoline)	(Account #)	(Phone Number)
(Gasoline)	(Account #)	(Phone Number)
(Store)	(Account #)	(Phone Number)
(Store)	(Account #)	(Phone Number)
(Store)	(Account #)	(Phone Number)
(Other)	(Account #)	(Phone Number)
(Other)	(Account #)	(Phone Number)

Stocks and Bonds

1. _____

   (Firm Name)   (Address)

   _____

   (Broker Name)   (Telephone)   (Account #)

   Shares/Stock Names: _____

   _____

   _____

   _____

2. _____

   (Firm Name)   (Address)

   _____

   (Broker Name)   (Telephone)   (Account #)

   Shares/Stock Names: _____

   _____

   _____

   _____

3. _____

   (Firm Name)   (Address)

   _____

   (Broker Name)   (Telephone)   (Account #)

   Shares/Stock Names: _____

   _____

   _____

   _____

Insurance Policies

Life _____   _____
       (Company Name)   (Policy Number)

      _____   _____
       (Agent Name)   (Phone Number)

House _____   _____
       (Company Name)   (Policy Number)

      _____   _____
       (Agent Name)   (Phone Number)

Auto _____   _____
       (Company Name)   (Policy Number)

      _____   _____
       (Agent Name)   (Phone Number)

Health _____   _____
       (Company Name)   (Policy Number)

      _____   _____
       (Agent Name)   (Phone Number)

Other _____   _____
       (Company Name)   (Policy Number)

      _____   _____
       (Agent Name)   (Phone Number)

The preceding pages give you the basic information you need to take absolute control of the family finances, or deny them to your wife. This also gives you a starting point if you decide to try to reduce your income for the coming year. We'll get into this more deeply in the section on family finances.

If you need to move out of the area, you may find that other companies provide basic services. Refuse pick-up, for example, is usually provided by the city, as is water. If you have an area selected, you ought to inform yourself regarding utilities there, to avoid a last-minute scramble while you already have enough on your plate.

Other types of services are movers and storage facilities. A few telephone calls can provide basic information, such as rates and locations. You can pick the ones you can afford, and zero in on those conveniently close to you. This shortens the list, and when the moment comes, you'll have saved some time.

Another aspect of being prepared is to have a nest-egg of your own, to provide you with ready cash if the situation becomes critical. You may need this urgently if your wife unexpectedly hits you with a court order. This means an untraceable source that's both safe and secret. One way is a private storage vault, which you rent for cash, to avoid any paper trail leading to it. Keep the key where your wife can't find it.

Utilities And Other Basic Services

Electricity _____   _____
(Company Name)   (Telephone)

_____   _____
(Address)   (Account #)

Gas   _____   _____
(Company Name)   (Telephone)

_____   _____
(Address)   (Account #)

Water _____   _____
(Company Name)   (Telephone)

_____   _____
(Address)   (Account #)

Refuse _____   _____
(Company Name)   (Telephone)

_____   _____
(Address)   (Account #)

Local Phone _____   _____
(Company Name)   (Telephone)

_____   _____
(Address)   (Account #)

Long Distance _____   _____
(Company Name)   (Telephone)

_____   _____
(Address)   (Account #)

Cable TV _____   _____
(Company Name)   (Telephone)

_____   _____
(Address)   (Account #)

Movers — Truck Rentals — Storage Facilities

1.

_____   _____
(Company Name)   (Telephone)

_____   _____
(Address)   (Rates/Notes)

2.

_____   _____
(Company Name)   (Telephone)

_____   _____
(Address)   (Rates/Notes)

3.

_____   _____
(Company Name)   (Telephone)

_____   _____
(Address)   (Rates/Notes)

4.

_____   _____
(Company Name)   (Telephone)

_____   _____
(Address)   (Rates/Notes)

5.

_____   _____
(Company Name)   (Telephone)

_____   _____
(Address)   (Rates/Notes)

6.

_____   _____
(Company Name)   (Telephone)

_____   _____
(Address)   (Rates/Notes)

Coping With Stress

You've probably had to cope with stress all of your life, especially because you're a man and a wage-earner. In our society, men still bear the heaviest burdens, despite the vicious feminist propaganda. Men still work to support the families, and men still fight the wars, despite a small skirmish by a few American female soldiers in the recent Panama War.

If you've been divorced before, drawing on your previous experience will help. Knowing that you have already survived a similar experience is reassuring. The emotional hardening you obtain from going through it once helps you cope with the next experience.

It also helps to have friends. "Friends" includes relatives with whom you have a close and trusting relationship. Emotional support during a crisis can be crucial.

Be prepared for a change in relationships with many people in your circle of friends and acquaintances. You'll soon see that they all fall into one of three groups:

1. Your friends, who remain loyal to you during the crisis. This doesn't necessarily mean that they'll become your wife's enemies, but that they will understand and support you.

2. Your wife's friends, who will be on her side. You may feel uncomfortable with these people, although they have not necessarily become your enemies.

3. Those who try to remain neutral or uninvolved. It's difficult to maintain neutrality, because of the risk of offending one party who may expect loyalty to his or her side. Some will react by creating distance in the relationship. You won't see them as often as previously, because they'll be "busy" with other things. Invitations to dinner

will stop, because of the awkwardness of inviting one partner without the other. Divorce can be a nasty business, and you can't blame anyone for refusing to take sides.

Sympathy also tends to go by sex, with the husband more likely to understand your viewpoint, and the wife remaining closer to your wife. You may have noticed this between yourself and your wife, when other couples you've known have split.

Among these people, you'll have to find one or two whom you can trust enough to discuss your problem. You may need to vent feelings, anxieties, and needs, and you also may need advice or tangible help from someone. A place to stay, the use of a car or truck, and other forms of direct help can help you cope during the first days of a split.

A psychologist who has been through divorce himself lists three types of help: friends, support groups, and professionals, in that order.[1] Friends are obviously the best choice, because they'll go the extra mile for you. Support groups are composed of strangers, who may be wary of getting too involved with you and your problems. Professionals, such as psychologists, psychiatrists, and various types of "counselors," are in it for the money. You may need someone with an M.D. to prescribe a tranquilizer, if you're into pills, but unless you've got a set of serious symptoms, stay away from them. You don't need to spend money on a hired ear when your cash is limited.

How do you decide which of your friends or acquaintances may want to help? One way is to consider those who have been through it themselves. Not having been divorced is not necessarily a disqualification, because some people are very understanding and empathetic, but a person who has had the experience knows what it's like because he's "been there."

Note the masculine pronoun. It's almost certain that you'll choose a male friend. Another man is likely to see it from your viewpoint, instead of automatically taking the wife's side. But, a woman might take your side, especially if she's unmarried and has a romantic interest in you.

If you can see it coming, start thinking about help from your best friend or friends. If you have a close friend with whom you can be totally honest, ask him for help before you need it. This may be a place to store some belongings during the crisis. Or you may want to use his truck in moving your goods. You may even need a place to stay for a few days in case you get locked out, or feel that leaving home is better than remaining. When soliciting help, make it clear that you're expecting only short-term help. You need to avoid suggesting that you may become a long-term burden, because this will strain a relationship. You also find out who your real friends are.

Sources

1. *Divorced Father*, Gerald A. Hill, Ph. D., White Hall, VA, Better Way Publications, 1989, p. 16.

6

Battle Plan Basics

It's hard to plan a course of action unless you have a framework, or a set of principles, to guide you. In civilian life, as well as in the military, strategy is all-important. The basics are similar, whatever the type of conflict. Let's go over the fundamentals:

Knowledge

This also goes by other names, such as "information," "intelligence," etc., which mean the same thing. You need to know what's happening. You have to inform yourself regarding the law, and your wife's intentions. You have to know her options, and that some of these are not open to you. She can, for example, obtain a court order throwing you out of the house because she's "afraid" of you, but you can't do the same to her.

Understanding your wife's mind-set can be very important. As we've noted above, there's a lot of feminist propaganda promoting a self-pitying attitude among women, and a viewpoint that men deserve whatever they get. Understanding this will help you avoid underestimating your wife's hatred and ruthlessness.

One very important point is whether or not she's having an affair, because this can affect the divorce settlement and have an even greater impact on the long-range outcome, as we'll see. Remember, adequate knowledge prevents your being surprised.

You also need to know the many small details that can make or break your plans. For example, do you keep a list of bank account numbers? Do you know whom to call to get the phone service transferred to your new residence? Do you know of a good divorce attorney? If not, find out, and record the information so that you'll have it when you need it.

Decision-making

There are two aspects to making decisions. One is to pre-program your decisions, considering all factors carefully before acting upon them. The formula goes like this:

"If....., then I'll.....

If ....., then I won't ......"

You can prepare a set of pre-packaged decisions well in advance, to cope with several possible sets of circumstances. This allows you to make more rational decisions, instead of being forced to make hurried ones in the heat of a difficult moment. We'll see how this works as we look into the range of choices you have in various situations.

The other aspect is to leave your options open as long as possible. This means that, although you may have decided on a course of action, you avoid making an irrevocable commitment until you really must. You need to do this because, often, you'll be acting on incomplete information. For example, you may suspect that your wife has a boyfriend, but may be unable to pin down the information. This means that you don't know whether or not you'll use this as grounds for divorce, in states which allow this, and until you can get the facts nailed down, you can't make an irrevocable commitment. It's smart to make preparations, but not take the final plunge until you're sure of your facts.

Preparation

Are you prepared? Deciding is one thing: acting upon it is another. The main point of preparation is to save you problems, work, and aggravation when you finally make your move. The more preparations you can make in advance, the less there will be to do at a time when you're over-worked and emotionally wrung out.

Initiative

Men have a weakness which women often exploit: they're more tolerant, laid-back, and willing to let things ride. If you're sitting back, waiting for things to happen, you're not in control of the situation. You have to make them happen.

The marriage oath contains the phrase: "for better or for worse," which some women use as an emotional blackjack against their husbands. These women convince their husbands to tolerate abuses because it's part of their role. If you're tolerating a bad marriage, playing it cool and hoping that it will get better, you're losing. You have to make your move, to grasp the initiative, and retain it. This is how you stay in control.

Limiting The Other's Options

This is the other side of decision-making. Maintaining control of the situation requires both keeping a wide range of choices open for yourself, and keeping your wife's options as narrow as possible. An example is restricting her freedom to move out by controlling the money. Another is to have the house, utilities, and cars in your name only.

As we've seen in Chapter Two, the roof can really fall in on a husband who allows his wife access to everything. A wife who can use her husband's money to finance her getaway, while driving him into bankruptcy, is dangerous.

Another way of restricting the wife's options is to force her to make certain moves. Keeping your set of keys when you move out forces her to have the locks changed, and the cost can be onerous if she doesn't have much spare cash.

Yet another way of limiting her options borders on psychological warfare. She's used it on you, and you can sometimes pay her back. You do it by setting up your ex-wife, her attorney, and the court with a no-win situation. For example, if your only valuable asset is the car you need for work, reduce your support payments. The other side faces the dilemma of seizing your car, which deprives you of your livelihood, or settling for lower payments and a promise to do better if your situation improves.

Priorities

Assigning priorities means not only considering first things first, but deciding what comes first. If you have to move out suddenly, what do you take? Do you take your shaving kit, wallet, checkbook, and clothing, or do you take your golf clubs and books? If there's a division of property, do you want to keep the house, car, boat, or country cabin? Is custody of the children negotiable in your state? If so, how many will you get? Can you care for them adequately? Making choices can be very difficult.

Another decision, as we'll see, is about the importance of obtaining information. Is your need to know so crucial as to justify the risk of her finding out that you're tapping the phone, going through her drawers, or opening her mail? That's a value judgment, which only you can decide.

Surprise

We've already seen how this factor can be tremendously important. However, surprise is a two-edged weapon. You need to avoid being surprised, such as coming home to find your belongings out on the sidewalk and the locks changed. You also can benefit from taking advantage of surprise, such as raiding the savings and checking accounts before she does it to you.

Surprise means taking the initiative. It means pre-empting, or striking first. Often, timing can make the difference between an easy divorce and an extraordinarily hard and painful one.

Unfortunately, it's the man who often gets surprised in a divorce. He may have been blissfully unaware that the ship was about to hit the sand, because he'd been too trusting. When he becomes aware, he's overwhelmed by the fast pace of the action once it starts. You need to avoid being surprised, for your own survival.

Possession

Keep in mind the old saying: "possession is nine-tenths of the law," as true today as it ever was. This is power politics in divorce, and forgetting it for a moment can be costly.

The basic principle is that if the furniture, car, or the bank accounts, are in your hands when the split comes, they're yours, for an unpredictable period of time. Even if your wife has an absolute claim to them, she can't regain possession until she takes the matter to court, and that can take a very long time.

You'll also see this if you move out of the house you own jointly with your wife. She gets to live rent-free, and if she has the locks changed, you can't return without breaking and entering. A court order can bar you from the area or premises. If you've left something behind, you'll have a problem.

Mobility

Being mobile makes you free. You get away from a bad situation by leaving the scene. Also moving targets are hard to hit. If you're concerned about court orders and support payments, one way to defend yourself is not to remain in one place long enough for your wife or a process server to find you.

Keeping Your Mental Balance

This can be very important, because divorce is a stressful event. At times, you may get the feeling that you're trying to keep too many balls in the air at once. It may also surprise you that some of your friends may see you as the bad guy in the relationship, because they sympathize with your wife. You need to learn how to cope with stress, and we'll cover this briefly later.

7

Get Sneaky

This chapter will teach you how to be sneaky. You'll need to have this knowledge under your belt, even if you're a straight-arrow, because you may become the victim of a few sneaky tricks. We've already studied some dishonest tactics wives use. Now we have to look at other sneaky ways they can work against you. If you understand the techniques, you'll be better able to protect yourself. Finally, you may have to use some sneaky tricks in self-defense.

Mail Drops

These are private postal addresses, operated to allow people to receive mail privately. Some people use mail drops for personal reasons, such as sexually-oriented correspondence. Others use them for business reasons, such as keeping accounts receivable away from the eyes and hands of employees.

A mail drop allows you to run a secret life. You can use a mail drop or a post office box to store your cash stash. You just put the money in an envelope and mail it to yourself at a box which you rent only for this purpose. Another use is to have bank account statements sent to your mail drop, to keep your wife in the dark. Remember that your wife may also have a mail drop.

Secrecy aside, a mail drop can serve a defensive purpose. Intercepting and destroying mail is a possibility when a marriage falls apart, especially with great animosity between partners. Today's postal service has deteriorated to the point that your wife can simply destroy mail addressed to you, and claim that it never arrived. She won't have any problem getting an attorney or judge to believe her. The only exception is mail requiring a signature.

If you get paid by mail, for example, you don't want your checks side-tracked. You may not want your wife to be able to open your envelopes and learn about your finances. If you run a business by mail, you may already be using a post office box. If any of your mail is important, protect it with a mail drop. Be sure to set this up before you move out, and make sure that all important correspondents have your new address.

Why a mail drop, and not a PO box? Actually, a post office box may do as well. There are, however, several problems with PO boxes. One is that there may not be one available at your nearby post office, because they're less costly than mail drops, and always in demand. Another is convenience. Post offices are not open at odd hours, and a mail drop, depending on the operator, may offer extended hours to pick up your mail. Check this point out carefully, though, because many post offices have public lobbies, open 24 hours a day, to allow post office box clients to pick up their mail at their convenience. The only problem remaining is if you receive "notified mail," which usually means a package too large to fit into the box, or a piece of mail requiring a signature. If you get to your box after hours, and find a notice inside, you'll have to come back during regular hours to pick up your mail.

Another convenience is that you can telephone ahead to the mail drop, to find out if anything has arrived for you. You need make a trip only if something has arrived. If you try this with the post office, they won't tell you "ZIP."

Many mail drops also offer forwarding services. You can use a mail drop in another city to give the impression that you're living there, even sending your outgoing mail to the operator to get that city's postmark. If you're planning to move out of state, and you use a mail drop to establish "residence" at your new location, this service can be very handy.

Finally, the post office will not accept package express for you. It has to be U.S. Mail or it doesn't get in the box. A private mail drop will accept anything, including UPS and Federal Express, and most don't charge extra for this service.

Costs may be important. A small post office box costs between ten and thirty dollars per year, with rates varying somewhat with demand. Mail drops vary even more, rates starting at about fifteen dollars for three months and going up to about thirty. The PO box cost includes a key. With mail drops, there's usually a three or five-dollar charge per key.

There are also charges for forwarding mail, including both handling and postage. This may be important, if you've decided to use a mail drop in another locale, and you can't go fetch your mail each day.

Finding a mail drop is easy today. This is a growth industry, and there's one in almost every town and neighborhood. The yellow pages list mail drops, under the "Mail Forwarding Service" classification. This is the most complete and reliable listing for mail drops in your area. However, if you need a mail drop outside your immediate area, you should consult the mail drop directory available from:

Loompanics Unlimited
PO Box 1197
Port Townsend, WA 98368

This lists mail drops in the United States, Canada, and several European countries. It's a worthwhile reference to use if you need a mail drop beyond your immediate area.

Another way to obtain a secret address is to take one over from a friend or fellow employee. Using someone else's mail box or drop is ideal, because there's absolutely nothing to connect it to you. This depends greatly on luck, but if you learn of someone who plans to move away, and to discontinue his mail drop or PO box, ask him for the key. He shouldn't mind, because maintaining the payments is entirely up to you. The Post Office or mail drop operator never dun a client for the fee. They simply collect payment in advance, and close the box if payment is late.

One advantage of using a European mail drop is that you can use it to send mail to the United States, to give the impression that you're living in a foreign country, in case you've decided to skip out on alimony payments. If this is your purpose, you should put a misleading return address on the envelope to be mailed from abroad, to avoid having it traced back to the mail drop. This technique is very useful to persuade your ex-wife and her attorney that you're beyond reach.

The Storage Room

Mini-storage depots have been a growth industry in the United States during the last couple of decades. Let's see how renting one can serve you before, during, and after a divorce.

The first step is keeping it secret from your wife. Obviously, you'll need to rent from an operator who doesn't know either of you, and therefore is unlikely to mention your rental to her in casual conversation. Another important point is to pay with cash, not a check. You don't want a canceled check revealing the rental if you have a joint account, or if you keep your bank records where she has access to them.

Also think about the key, if you secure the door to the storage room with a padlock. If your wife's the nosy type, you'd better hide it, or use a combination lock.

The storage room provides a secret place for financial records, tangible assets, illegal substances, and other material you may want to keep from your wife. If your secret hobby is cross-dressing, keep your second wardrobe in the storage room. Finally, the room is a convenient place for temporary storage once you decide to move out. It enables you to transfer your possessions gradually, in small amounts, to avoid alerting her that you're planning a break.

The Storage Vault

This is a private safe-deposit box, offering even more security for you. The reason for using a private vault is that bank safe-deposit boxes are under the thumb of the federal and state governments. Banks, and savings & loan associations, are closely regulated, and some of the regulations deal with safe deposit boxes. This is why IRS investigators, in case of suspected tax irregularities, search for safe deposit boxes. They can find them, if they're in banks.

State laws can also cause you certain problems. In many states, upon your death the bank will close your box until an auditor and an official from the state tax office can go over the contents. If you keep anything in your box that you want another person, such as a special friend or business associate, to have upon your death, they won't have access to it.

A private vault company doesn't fall under this sort of regulation, and can be pretty discreet. In fact, discretion is their business. Like storage-room operators, they can rent to whom they please, without any requirement for reporting their clients to any government agency. In practice, a private vault is a safe place to stash cash, bank-books, credit cards, and checkbooks. The advantage is that the private vault company provides a lot more security, for small objects, than the storage-room operator.

Telephone Tapping

Today, it's easier than ever to eavesdrop on a telephone conversation. This is something to keep in mind when you decide to speak about a sensitive subject on the phone.

Listening in can be as easy as picking up the extension. You have to watch your breathing, which can be heard over the set. If you intend to listen in on an extension, you can unscrew the mouthpiece and remove the microphone, to make sure that inadvertent sounds won't give you away.

If you have a cordless phone, you can buy another handset, allowing you to listen without even a "click" as you tune in. An advantage of the cordless phone is that you can leave the house and listen in from many yards away, if you suspect that your wife is about to make a significant call. The U.S. Supreme Court has recently ruled that any eavesdropper may listen in to a cordless phone conversation, even without a warrant.

Recording is almost as easy, with the advantage that you don't have to be physically present to monitor the line. A telephone recording control, and a voice-activated tape recorder, (VOX) are all you need. The recording control is available at Radio

Shack for less than fifteen dollars, and VOX recorders are available almost anywhere for fifty dollars or less.

The recording control has to be connected in series with the telephone. This means that the telephone's jack goes into the black box, and the box's wire and jack lead to the wall plug. If you have more than one telephone, it won't work from the extension, unless you pick up the handset. If you can wire the recording control box to the telephone lead-in to your home, you can have a series connection.

The other choice, if you have more than one phone, is to put the control box in series with the telephone your wife usually uses. For this, you have to hide it and the recorder well. If a table or other furniture screens the telephone wall outlet from view, you may be able to put the control box in series. If, however, your wife walks around with the phone in her hand while carrying on a conversation, she may wind up dragging the tape recorder behind her. Likewise, if she decides to dust under the table. Everything has its risks, and you have to decide which risks are worth taking.

One-party Recording

In many states, it's legal for one party to record a telephone conversation without informing the other. This can lead to a trap for the unwary or the indiscreet. This concerns you if you become involved in a telephone conversation with your wife after you've left. In principle, you should have your attorney handle all communications, but she may call to try to goad you into making statements to use against you. This is why you should assume that all telephone conversations with your wife are being recorded.

A simple and effective way to handle the problem is not to get into any discussions with her. Don't agree to anything, and don't answer any questions. If she telephones you, tell her that, if she has any questions or comments, she should put them to your attorney. The other side of the coin is to keep a tape recorder connected to your telephone, in case she makes any indiscreet admissions.

Silence and Secrecy

Once you've decided that you want a divorce, be especially discreet. You don't want to tip your hand, and you don't want to frighten your wife into acting first. Play for time, because once you've decided to act, time may not be on your side. You'll need several weeks, and you'll need a schedule to guide you.

Be careful regarding whom you tell. You may feel the need to "unload," to vent your feelings, but choose your audience carefully. The person whom you think is a "friend" may be more friendly with your wife than with you, and leak the news. Also, choose a discreet person, not the office or neighborhood gossip, who may blab your secret recklessly.

If you absolutely have to vent your feelings, but don't know whom to trust, hire a shrink. This is generally poor advice if you really need help, but for a casual talk, you can survive the experience. The fee you pay binds him to secrecy. Another possibility is your attorney, if he's truly your attorney and not the family lawyer. Make sure that you pay him, though, to legally establish the "attorney-client relationship." This means, in theory, that he can be disbarred for violating your confidence.

Discretion also applies to two especially damaging types of speech; threats and more threats. Never threaten your wife with violence, or strike her, especially in front of witnesses. Also, never make statements that can return to haunt you, especially in the heat of an argument. For example, if you're arguing about alimony, don't ever, ever, ever threaten to reduce your income to jeopardize her alimony payments. This is an option you may keep in reserve, but never speak about it. She can use it against you in court.

Dodging Payments

The outcome of a trial depends more on the quality of each side's presentation, and the judge's prejudices, than on who is actually "right" or "wrong." If your wife has a better lawyer than yours, or if the judge is biased towards women, you may find yourself getting economically raped in the courtroom.

A factor in your favor is that your wife's attorney, if at all competent, will have explained to her that receiving payments depends on your cooperation, and that crippling payments are excellent incentives for running out on them. It boils down to loading the contingencies, and a piece of paper known as a "court order" won't amount to a hill of beans if you decide not to obey it. This is the same problem facing wives with truly violent husbands. A "peace bond," or restraining order, won't stop a man with a burning anger against his wife. Some wives have been severely beaten, and even killed, by husbands who didn't care if they went to jail. One angry husband shot his wife to death in church, before killing himself.

Consider the prospect of payments that make life just about impossible for you. The drain on your resources becomes so onerous that you conclude that obeying the law is merely a sucker's game. You feel that you have nothing to lose by defying the court's judgment. You may also decide that, no matter what comes, your ex-wife is not going to benefit from the court judgment. If you decide to resist regardless of disruption of your life-style, you're in the driver's seat. Your ex-wife can't possibly win, because all you have to do, is to do nothing.

At this time, let's repeat one crucial point: If this is your intent, say nothing about it to anybody! No attorney or judge will accept any excuse, if forewarned that you had intended to act in bad faith. If you declare that you're going to reduce your income, or use other tactics, you'll get slapped into jail right away. If, on the other hand, you present a credible picture of a sincere individual who has been dogged by bad luck, your ex-wife will have to endure the frustration of watching you waltz around while she has to eat her heart out waiting for her checks.

One intermediate step, before deciding on the final bug-out, is to stop making payments and see what happens. You can stall, make partial payments, and use a whole gamut of delaying tactics to deprive your ex-wife of the fruits of her victory. There is a repertory of excuses you can use:

- Your check is in the mail.

- My income was down this month.

- A lot of people who owe me money haven't paid me.

- My car broke down and it cost a lot to repair.

- I'm waiting for a large check to clear.

- I've been off work because of illness.

You can avoid payments by reducing your income or getting yourself fired. This is easy, and only a grave error on your part will give you away. Begin by taking time off from work because of "illness," to use up any sick leave you have accrued. You must, however, remain at home, watching TV, and not make a spectacle of yourself going to shows, or to the beach, when you're allegedly home "sick."

You or your attorney can easily make a good case that your health has taken a down-turn after the divorce. You can claim to have acquired one virus after another, a series of illnesses, because the short flu is quick in both onset and recovery. During winter, you've got the weather going for you.

If you claim illness from short-acting flu, you're unlikely to have consulted a doctor about each attack. This is perfectly credible, and if your income is entirely from a job, you can pay your ex-wife little or nothing, and get away with it for a long time. If you're absent from work enough, your employer will sooner or later replace you.

Once you're unemployed, payments to your ex-wife will have to come from your unemployment check, which is usually modest. Benefits vary from state to state. They're typically just enough to pay the rent and buy a starvation diet. They also don't last longer than six months. As an unemployed person, you can ask the court for a temporary reduction or suspension of alimony payments.

While you're ill or out of work, you can nevertheless enjoy a fairly comfortable life. If you have a stash of cash, it will pay for some expensive pleasures. A few changes of clothing and a cash box, safely stored in a storage room, can provide you with the means for a few glorious weekends. If your ex-wife, or the court, asks why you were not at home, you can say that you spent a weekend with a gallon of "Mad Dog 20-20," and were sleeping on a park bench.

Another way to have a good time is to enjoy the generosity and hospitality of friends. If you have friends who enjoy your company, they can provide you with dinners and mini-vacations, all out of reach of the court. Your ex-wife may have to make do with a frozen dinner, while you eat steak and lobster as your friends' guest. You may also get invited to accompany them on vacations, without cost to you.

If you play your hand adeptly, you can spin it out for weeks or months. Regardless of the court's order, you can deprive your ex-wife of payments for a long time before it catches up to you. If called to explain your default to a judge, adopt a humble attitude and say something like:

"I'm trying to pay, your honor, but I've been sick." If he threatens you with jail, simply say:

"I know my payments have been late, your honor, but if I go to jail, I'll lose my job, and won't be able to pay anything."

Excuses go only so far. Theoretically, the judge can hit you for "contempt of court," and send you to jail until you cough up the money. Judges are reluctant to do this, because if in jail, you can't earn money for payments. In most cases, therefore, the judge won't send you to jail unless you anger him. If he views your behavior as a personal affront, he can easily put you behind bars.

Finally, you may decide that it's time for the comedy to end. You're sick and tired of the hassle, and feel that you're in a no-win situation. This means bugging out, overtly or covertly.

Escape and Evasion

You may find life after divorce too difficult if your wife has crippled you financially, and decide to bug out without leaving a forwarding address. You also might decide to move out of state, knowing that you can do so legally, because it'll be a hassle for your wife to track you down.

It's extremely difficult to avoid being found if there's a major national effort to find you. If, for example, you were a Soviet spy on the run, every police agency in the country would have your description, and you might be recognized by any traffic cop or highway patrolman. FBI Agents would be combing hotels, motels, airports, bus stations, and even flop-houses, to locate you.

If you're ducking a civil judgment, the court won't enlist the police, FBI, and Interpol to find you. This country's high crime rate is in your favor. Each year, the cops have to cope with about

20,000 homicides, half a million armed robberies, and over 3 million burglaries.

Police have computerized networks to trace wanted persons, and each time a traffic cop stops an offender, he checks him out for "wants." These are only interstate felony warrants, and misdemeanor and traffic warrants within the state. You may have several outstanding traffic and parking tickets, but if you're stopped in another state, they won't check these out. A civil matter, such as defaulting on alimony payments, doesn't go into the crime computer.

Let's consider some hypothetical examples:

■ You're a journeyman carpenter, a union member specializing in construction, and you work from one construction job to another. You can easily move to another job out of state, earn several weeks' pay there, and move on to another when the job ends. Right after your divorce, you leave to work in an adjacent state, without sending your ex-wife any alimony. You make no effort to conceal your whereabouts. She tells her lawyer to complain to the judge, but by the time the court locates you and takes any action, you're gone. Stymied, your ex-wife tries to find your new location. Her lawyer helps by hiring a private detective, but before the court can act, you've moved on to another job. A moving target is very hard to hit!

■ You've stashed enough cash to support you for a year, and you immediately take off for parts unknown. Although you travel under your own name, and don't make any effort to change your identity, you are also careful not to leave a paper trail to lead anyone to you. You pay for everything in cash, to avoid leaving credit card receipts. You travel by train and bus, to avoid leaving a name with an airline ticket clerk. You travel about the country, staying in motels no longer than three days at a time, and you spend several nights with friends. Your ex-wife and her lawyer have absolutely no trace of you, and don't even know whether you're dead or alive. You do, however, keep her attorney informed that you're still in the land of the living, by sending him letters post-marked from different parts of the country every few weeks.

■ You don't have much cash, and only a second-hand car and a couple of suitcases of clothing. You abandon your job, and set off to take menial jobs where you find them, giving a false name and social security number to each employer. You live modestly, often sleeping in your car to save the price of a motel room, because working as a day laborer and dishwasher doesn't bring in much money. Several times, police see you sleeping in your car and check you out, but as you're not wanted on any felony warrants, they let you go after checking I.D. Your ex-wife's lawyer may suspect that you have been working at odd jobs around the country, but he hasn't been able to catch up to you.

■ Your work doesn't tie you to a particular geographical area, and you buy a motor home. Your itinerary takes you from state to state. Completely self-contained, you travel from one trailer park to another, never staying in the same place for more than a week at a time. You pay cash, to avoid leaving a paper trail. You use a mail drop in one state to receive your mail, which you pick up at irregular intervals, when you happen to be in the area.

■ You've seen it coming for a couple of years, and decided not to make a move until you were good and ready. You've earned enough to stash money in a couple of foreign bank accounts, and you have your passport ready. Once the divorce decree is final, you step on an airplane and you're gone. You tease your ex-wife by sending an occasional postcard from abroad, mailing one in each country the day you're about to leave. Her lawyer advises her to give up trying, as there's no chance of extradition for failure to pay alimony, even if they could catch you.

■ You've seen it coming, and decided to do a total vanishing act. You've opened a savings account under another name, in another state. Piece by piece, you've procured a new set of I.D.

based on the birth certificate of someone who died in infancy, as described in many books on generating new I.D.[1] The day the punitive divorce decree comes through, you're out of there, and nobody ever sees you again. You live in another part of the country, under another name, and may even remarry and raise a family.

Many genuine vanishing acts are the result of marital discord.[2] To do this successfully requires both a certain state of mind and technical knowledge.

Also important is timing. One authority makes a good case for vanishing before the divorce.[3] The advantages of leaving before the divorce are that you save money otherwise needed to pay the lawyer, and spent in moving the conventional way. The wife suffers because her legal status remains unclear, without either a divorce decree or death certificate. She cannot sell any jointly-owned property, collect on life insurance, and she must pay any taxes or debts on the property, or face eviction.

If you decide to disappear, you have to learn to live undercover. To succeed, you must not leave a trail. If, for example, you work for the government, including the armed forces, or collect social security, veteran's benefits, etc., these will lead to your door. If you file income tax returns and social security payments under your real name or social security number, tracing you becomes a piece of cake. There are other leads which can disclose your whereabouts to a vengeful ex-wife. A checklist of important points to watch is the following:

- Do not use a moving company to move your stuff to your new address. This creates a direct line to you, and a private investigator can easily trace you this way. The best way is to travel light, and carry everything in your vehicle.

- Break off all contacts with friends and relatives in your former life. These are the people whom investigators will approach in the hope of finding your whereabouts. They may use ruses such as "Mr. Jones inherited $100,000 and we're trying to find him to give him the check." Another investigator's trick is to send you a check for a small amount, and if it gets forwarded and you deposit it in your account, the investigator has your bank and account number. One book, written by a female advocate, suggests that the wife should try to pump her husband's relatives and friends for information, and advises the ex-wife to be "chatty."[4]

- Don't leave a forwarding address with anyone, even if it's only a mail drop. There are ways of tracing you even from these. An elementary way, if you file a change-of-address with your post office, is to send you a certified letter with a return tag, requesting SHOW ADDRESS WHERE DELIVERED.

- Avoid even telephone calls, because the new electronic equipment used by the telephone company allows a trace in seconds. This precaution is only if an official agency is interested in you. If you absolutely need to make a telephone call to an old friend or relative, use a telephone booth far from your new home.

- Use a phony social security number on all paperwork, such as driver's license applications and employment records. Also use a wrong number on your income tax return.

- Don't register to vote.

- Avoid having a telephone, if possible. If you must have one, do it under another name.

- Avoid giving real information to interviewers who compile city directories. Appear cooperative, to avoid raising suspicions, but lie like hell.

- Do not transfer subscriptions for publications. You may subscribe, but only to a mail drop, and only under another name. Best of all, buy them on the news-stand.

- Discontinue contact or membership in clubs and associations, because your ex-wife may contact these to seek your whereabouts.

- If you're in an occupation that requires licensing, such as medicine, law, dentistry, etc., consider changing your line of work or moving to another country. State licensing bureaus are leads to your whereabouts.

- Use your mail drop address for everything, including your new driver's license.

- Don't apply for any credit cards. Use cash instead. This limits your ability to rent a car, for example, but you can get by without this.

- Travel by inter-urban bus, or by train, to avoid leaving a name. If you must fly, remember that airlines don't check I.D., and you can use an alias.

- Consider living in a city with good public transport, to avoid the need for a car, driver's license, insurance, etc.

- Keep a low profile, such as avoiding driving a large and opulent car, wearing expensive or loud clothes, etc. Also avoid attracting notice, such as conducting loud parties.

- Avoid getting arrested for petty offenses, such as drunk driving, and don't get involved with avoidable hazards, such as illegal drugs.

Your chances of remaining free are better than you might think. We've already seen that cops always put a civil matter on the back burner. Even when a publicity-hungry judge starts a campaign against child-support defaulters, he can only act against those he can reach. This means only those living in the same state and county, and who are making no effort to hide.

To gain a good perspective of how the odds favor you, unless you do something stupid, consider the fate of serial murderers in this country. There have been several noted ones, such as

Lucas, Bundy, Corrl, and Gacy, caught only after they'd been killing for years. A homicide takes top priority with police agencies, and when there's evidence of a serial murderer operating, state police and the FBI get into the investigation. Sometimes, the investigation peters out, despite their best efforts. The "Green River Killer," in the Pacific Northwest, is still at large after years of work, and the Green River Task Force is dying out as participating agencies are transferring officers into more promising investigations.

The basic principle here is that a serial killer is often a moving target. Most who have been caught have operated from the same home base for years. Some were discovered only when the stink of rotting bodies aroused neighbors to complain. Others, such as Dean Corrl, were killed by a victim.

Skip tracers live on their reputations, because in reality most are lazy and incompetent.[5] In tracing people, they rely on the fact that most people who skip are not savvy, and make basic mistakes that leave a trail right to their doorsteps. It's often enough to trace someone by his social security number, to find out where he's currently working, for example. They collect their fees "up front," and do not guarantee results. The danger of being tracked down by one of these, despite the occasional success story, is minimal.

Clandestine Money Handling

Money laundering can be a tricky task. You need a source of ready cash that is both handy for you, and absolutely out of reach of your wife, her attorney, or the court. This means that you need to store money where it won't be available to your wife, won't show up on official documents, and won't leave a paper trail leading to you or your activities. Remember, any separate savings or checking account you have may show up on your income tax return. Even if you don't list it, to avoid alerting your wife, the bank sends a Form 1099 to the IRS.

Let's examine closely the ins and outs of clandestine money dealing. First, forget about using credit cards, as these simply lay a paper trail directly to you, unless you've been able to establish a credit card account under a different identity. Also forget about using checks, because these often require supporting documents, such as a driver's license and a major credit card, to be accepted by retailers and hotel personnel.

There are two ways of going about providing money for clandestine purposes. One is the quick and dirty way, which has the advantages of being effective on short-notice, and does not involve you in complications, such as fake I.D. You simply stash your cash in a safe-deposit box in a private storage vault. If you travel around the country on business, you can leave cash stashes in several cities.

This provides money to rent an apartment, storage room, or vault. Don't use your regular checking account, because it would show up under the most casual inspection. A check paying for an apartment rental, for example, would give your plan away, as would a canceled check from a storage or vault company. One way to keep such payments out of your checking account statement is to use money orders. These are as good as cash when renting a mail drop in another city, and in fact, an international money order will rent you a mail drop in another country. However, buy it with cash, not with a check.

The other way is to set up a new identity, and use that to establish bank accounts in several places. The advantage of this method is that your money isn't simply in cold storage, but can be earning interest for you. This is important to help offset the effects of inflation. You'll find that banks now require you to show I.D. to open an account, or face the prospect of having a percentage of any interest you earn amputated and turned over to the IRS as a precaution to ensure that the government gets its share. You can provide a fake social security number, and by the time the bureaucracy gets around to inquiring about the discrepancy, you'll have closed the account and moved the money elsewhere.

Sources

1. One excellent reference book on arranging both the paperwork and the disappearance is *How to Disappear Completely and Never Be Found*, Doug Richmond, Port Townsend, WA, Loompanics Unlimited, 1986. This is a "how-to" manual that covers both procuring the paperwork and engineering the disappearance.

   Another, written from a slightly different slant, is *How to Get Lost and Start All Over Again*, Gary B. Clark, Port Townsend, WA, Loompanics Unlimited, 1986. This book gets into economic problems deeply, and examines questions such as finding a new job, filing bankruptcy, and other topics that are strictly economic.

   New I.D. In America, by Anonymous, Boulder, CO, Paladin, 1983, is a nuts and bolts text on the mechanics of obtaining a new official identity by "paper tripping."

2. *How to Disappear Completely and Never Be Found*, p. 9.

3. *Ibid.*, p. 13.

4. *Child Support*, Marianne Takas, New York, Harper & Row, 1985, p. 58.

5. An acquaintance of the author's was tracked down by long-lost relatives who had hired a private investigator to search for him. Although this person had always existed under the same name, had never made any attempt to hide or change identities, always lived in a major metropolitan area, and was even listed in the telephone directory, the

private investigator said that he'd had a hell of a hard time finding him.

8

Judicial Jujitsu

Although laws vary from state to state, many practices and procedures remain the same. In this section, we'll take a look at some of the pitfalls, traps, and problems you may expect.

Injunctions, Summonses, and Lockouts

"Domestic violence" has become a catch phrase during the past decade. A few well-publicized and sensationalized cases of wife-beating have led to various laws to protect wives from physical abuse by their spouses. This means you!

If you've beaten your wife, especially in front of witnesses or severely enough to send her to the hospital, you can expect little mercy. In fact, the odds are that you will have been arrested, if you live in a state with severe domestic violence laws. Police practice is also hardening, leading to arrests in family disturbances.

Physical force against a wife is a serious tactical error, with repercussions beyond any jail time you might serve. In states which still have divorce for cause, it counts against you in court. Even in "no fault" states, you can find it rough going if you are before a female judge, or one who hates wife-beaters.

This can also work against you if you have never struck or threatened your wife. The way the law is actually applied, in many states a wife can go before a judge, and claim she fears for her safety, that her husband has threatened her, etc., and obtain an "ex parte" order for her "protection." "Ex parte" means that you are not consulted or given a hearing before the judge issues the order. You will get your day in court, but only after a few days or weeks. "Justice delayed is justice denied," because in the meantime, you have to move out. If you try to return home, you face jail.

Normal procedure is that, within ten days or a similar short period, you'll get a chance to tell your side to the judge who issued the order. The problem with this is that it's often your word against your wife's. Basically, she can lie like hell, you can't prove that she's lying, and the judge will usually accept her version. This is especially true if the judge is a feminist, or is afraid of antagonizing the feminists in the community.

Injunctions and summonses serve other purposes. One is to tie up your finances so that you can't relocate. Another is to make it difficult for you to pay an attorney. A court order mandating that you turn over all bank accounts, checkbooks, credit cards, etc., is a possibility. More likely is an order forbidding you to make any withdrawals except for normal living expenses.

To make the court order effective, it must be "served" upon you, or upon your authorized agent, by a process server. Some people believe that, if you can avoid the process server, you can avoid the court order. Not so. The process server doesn't need to make physical contact with you and place the paper in your hand. Many states have laws allowing service by mail, and service by proxy. A process server can give the summons to your attorney, if you have one, and this counts as if he'd placed it in your hand. If you have a mail drop, sending it by certified mail, requiring a signature from the mail drop operator, is adequate to satisfy the law. If you live in a state still requiring service in person, you may think you can avoid the process server by never opening your door to a stranger. Not necessarily. The law may allow him to leave it on your doorstep, after advising you of his identity and purpose.

Your Attorney

There are many nasty jokes about attorneys:

An attorney went swimming in shark-infested waters, but didn't get bitten. Why not?

Answer: Professional courtesy.

Another attorney died and went to heaven. Saint Peter met him at the gate, and informed him that the Presidential Suite would be ready for him in about ten minutes, and invited him to take a seat in the waiting area. While the attorney was waiting, he saw the Pope, who had just died, come to the gate. Saint Peter told him: "Oh, yeah, Pope, we'll put you in Dormitory H."

The attorney got up and asked Saint Peter why the Pope was getting a bed in a dormitory, while he, a mere attorney, was getting a suite all by himself. Saint Peter answered:

"Well, I've got 75 popes up here, but you're the only attorney who ever made it."

Another attorney comes to the pearly gates, protesting that there must be an error, because he's only 38 years old, and too young to die. Saint Peter asks him to wait, while he checks the record book. Upon returning, Saint Peter tells him:

"Well, I checked our records, and according to hours billed, you're 86 years old."

Attorneys have been getting very bad press lately, much of which comes from doctors who resent being held responsible for their carelessness and neglect. This propaganda is effective, persuading some people that anyone who becomes a lawyer is an unethical slimeball. In reality, there are good and bad lawyers, just as there good and bad doctors, grocers, mechanics, etc.

Like doctors, lawyers often specialize. Some are criminal lawyers, while others do corporate law. There are family practitioners, and even divorce specialists.

Just as they vary in specialties and abilities, they also vary in fees they charge. Fees don't necessarily correspond with skill, which is exactly the same situation as we find with doctors, mechanics, and other tradesmen.

One point to keep in mind, though, is that attorneys bill by the hour, and that, like a taxi driver, your attorney has a vested interest in keeping the meter running. Keep this in mind at every point, because you may find it's cheaper to make a concession in your case than to spend twice as much on attorney's fees fighting it in court. Beware of the lawyer who wants to fight every minor point out in court.

What sort of attorney do you want or need? There are various opinions on this, but one fact is clear: if you intend to work through "the system," you do need one. Why? Let's look at several good reasons.

Respect

This is perhaps the most important reason of all. It may not be possible to discuss or negotiate with your wife, because she won't respect you. If every conversation deteriorates into a confrontation, and every discussion into a name-calling session, you need a third party to handle it for you. A professional person, such as an attorney, can get her attention and make her listen, partly because he's not directly involved in the conflict, and partly because he's got the prestige.

The other side of respect is the attitudes of judges and other attorneys towards laymen. Lawyers are members of an exclusive club, and outsiders are not welcome. Have you ever been to court, for any reason, and noticed the dismissive attitudes shown to defendants? Have you noticed how impatient judges become when listening to laymen? Have you ever heard a judge interrupt a layman and announce his verdict? Fact is, judges and attorneys look down upon laymen, and see them as a lesser breed of human. They adopt the same patronizing attitude doctors often show towards their patients. If you have an attorney representing you, he'll act as their equal, but on your behalf, up to a point.

Professional Knowledge

This is another important reason. You may read the divorce and property statutes in your state, but do you know exactly what they mean, and how courts are currently interpreting them? It's easy to misunderstand fundamental facts when you get into a specialized field. It's worse if you're in a highly emotional situation, and substitute wishful thinking for solid fact. You may think that you have certain rights, when in fact you don't. You may think that a certain law is valid and still in force, without knowing that a Supreme Court decision struck it down the week before.

Objectivity

A clear head is important in a divorce. It's an emotional situation, and you may not see things clearly. You need a second pair of eyes on the facts, to help and advise you.

Don't always count on friends for advice. They're on your side, and will probably agree with everything you say. In an emotional moment, they may hesitate to contradict you, even if they suspect you're mistaken. This is why a genuine third party can help you understand the ramifications and make decisions.

Choosing An Attorney

Finding an attorney can be hit-or-miss. The yellow pages provide listings and advertisements, but all you'll find out is attorneys' specialties. Look for "family relations" or "divorce," but also check out any prospective choice by looking at the other categories. If a lawyer is listed as a specialist in divorce, criminal law, drunk driving, and wills, he can't be much of a specialist.

The local bar association can provide a list of lawyers who specialize in family practice or divorce. You can get the same information from the yellow pages. You may also get some names from a "lawyer's referral service." As with referrals from the bar association, these services simply hand out the names of members, regardless of their competence. If you have to go in "cold," try to see a few attorneys who offer free first sessions.

This will give you an opportunity to size up each one, and try to make a choice.

One type to avoid is the attorney who rushes you, because he may be running a divorce mill, putting your case on the assembly line with many others. Also watch out for the one who hands you over to a junior partner in his firm. This tells you that you're going to get the second or third team representing you.

Another type to avoid, unless you're sure that your case is rock-solid, is the city or county attorney with a practice on the side. This type will be more concerned about his official standing and reputation than with the needs of his clients. He'll be reluctant to "judge shop" because of the risk of antagonizing a judge before whom he'll have to appear in his official capacity. On the other hand, if your case is legally defensible, he may be able to do a better job for you because of his contacts. He's also less likely to pad his bill, or cheat you in other ways.

Recommendations from friends can help. A friend who says he "got a great deal" with one attorney may actually be giving you bad advice, because the same attorney may not be able to work the same miracle in your case. However, if a friend warns you about an attorney with whom he had a bad experience, this is worth noting.

Once you decide that you need a divorce specialist, you still have to decide upon his skill and personal qualities. The yellow pages won't give you a clue about these. What sort do you need? The answer depends upon whom you ask. Some will advise getting a tough negotiator, who can wring the most concessions in your favor out of a divorce settlement. That's one viewpoint.

Another viewpoint is to seek an attorney who himself has been divorced. Presumably, he'll have more sympathy for you. However, this may not be good logic. If you're suffering from a cardiac condition, you wouldn't necessarily seek a doctor who himself has had a heart attack. A corollary to this is not to hire an attorney whose religious views frown on divorce. A devout Roman Catholic or Mormon is likely to be "down" on divorce, and may not do the best job for you.

Yet another way is to get one with a lot of experience in handling divorces. The reason for this is obvious. You don't want a criminal lawyer handling a divorce case, any more than you'd want a corporation lawyer representing you on a criminal charge. The ability to negotiate well is important, and we'll cover this presently.

Some people feel that a good divorce attorney should not only be a tough negotiator, but an unethical sleazeball, to collaborate with his client on various legal and illegal dodges to secure advantages in the property settlement. One way to do so is to conceal assets. Nevertheless, keep one important point in mind, if you're trying to find a lawyer to be your co-conspirator in shady dealings.

If his ethics are deficient, he may also be screwing you. There are many ways lawyers can cheat their clients. One is to overcharge. Although you may request an estimate of the costs at the outset, a dishonest lawyer is like a cab driver who takes the long way round to run up mileage on the meter. He may mis-state the hours he spends on your case. He may also encourage you to go for more than you can reasonably expect in negotiations with your spouse, knowing that the more time he runs up on the meter, the more money he'll get from you. The bottom line is that, any lawyer who will accept or encourage illegal behavior is a very dangerous person to hire.

Try to get a feel for whether the lawyer will give you personal attention, or just run your case through a mass-production operation. Also try to get a feel for whether his sympathies are with you or with your wife. Listen to the way he questions you about your situation. Is he playing "devil's advocate," trying to see it the way the court would see it, or does he show disapproval of you or the way you've handled the matter so far?

Also watch out for the lawyer with a "rah-rah" attitude, who cheers you on with promises of overwhelming victory in court. He may be simply leading you on, expecting you to authorize extensive litigation. As he gets paid by the hour, he gains whether you win or lose.

The best type of lawyer is the one who will discuss frankly the pros and cons of your case. No case is perfect, and you may stand to win in one aspect, and not do as well in another. Your lawyer should make you aware of your case's strong and weak points, to help you decide the best way to go.

You have to decide. Never forget that it's your decision and your ultimate responsibility. Your lawyer is working for you, not the other way around. It has to be your ultimate decision because you're the one who will have to live with the consequences, not he.

A serious mistake made by many people who need attorneys is that they don't try before they buy. An interview in the lawyer's office, or a friend's recommendation, often isn't enough, but test-driving an attorney isn't like test-driving a car.

One way of getting an impression of what sort of job an attorney will do for you is to watch him in action. If you can take the time, advises Richard Templeton, of America's Society of Separated and Divorced Men, attend domestic relations court and watch how each attorney handles himself in court. If you've already chosen a lawyer, ask him when he'll next appear in court to represent a client in a divorce, then go watch how he conducts himself on behalf of his client. Does he truly fight, or is he a wimp? Does he cross-examine with incisiveness and verve, or is he as impressive as a wet noodle?

If you don't yet have a lawyer, attend court to form an impression of attorneys appearing. If you see one you like, approach him outside the court and ask for an interview. At least, you'll have the priceless advantage of trying before buying.

Don't decide on price alone. The worst kind of attorney you can get, if you're facing anything but a sweet and purely amicable divorce, is the one who runs a mass-production divorce clinic. These process their clients in a purely routine way, and you often don't get service worth the little you pay for it. The hourly rate may be lower, but they charge for "expenses," which means that you wind up paying the same, anyway. If they nickel-and-dime you with a plethora of routine "expenses," such as having papers typed and photocopied, you'll end up paying more.

Finally, begin looking for an attorney long before you need one. By this stage, you should understand the value of advance preparation, and the difficulty of trying to make last-minute decisions when under stress. Visit divorce court to scout the territory and watch lawyers in action. Listen to recommendations from friends. Check out any lawyers who seem worth following up, long before your situation goes critical.

Working With an Attorney

Let's look at an important fact about the way attorneys work and think, because it's important not to expect too much. Lawyers are members of a cozy little club, and their main loyalty is to the system in which they work, not to you, the client. Your wife's lawyer is also an attorney. So is the judge. Your lawyer knows that he'll have to return and work with these people again and again, but that you're only one client. His relationship with you is not as important as his relationship with them.[1]

This is why there may be a certain amount of low-key deception at your expense. Your attorney may be long on promises, but short on performance. He may not tell you in so many words that he can obtain a certain outcome for you, but he'll lead you to believe that he can by making exaggerated claims in the official papers he files. They'll get shot down in court, but at least he can show you that he tried. He may also write bombastic letters to the other lawyer, not expecting that they'll be taken seriously, but only to impress you with the belief that he's solidly on your side. This is why you have to take everything with a grain of salt.

It should be very clear at the outset that your attorney is working for you. Your spouse may or may not choose to hire her own, but you always should do so. The one you hire is your attorney, and his priority is to look out for your interests. Don't think that the lawyer can effectively wear two hats. He can't really be both yours and your spouse's at the same time. It's important to stress this point because some couples try to save money by having one attorney do the work of two. This can only work if both parties are fairly agreeable, and are parting amicably. In such a case, they agree on the splitting of the property and other matters beforehand, and the lawyer just shuffles the papers. If there's any animosity between spouses, though, there will be problems.

The other side of the coin is that, if you try to get along with only one attorney, make sure that he's your attorney, not your spouse's. If she's naive enough to agree, so be it. Take advantage of that fact, and make sure that your attorney understands that he's working for you, not her. He's under no obligation to advise her of her rights, or to see that she gets a "fair" share of the settlement.

Your relationship with your lawyer will have a lot to do with how successful he'll be in protecting your interests. If you have a good lawyer, you can come out of the affair without losing your shirt. To do this, however, you must also do your part. Tell him everything he needs to know, and follow his recommendations. If you don't, you're wasting his time and your money.

One awful mistake you must avoid is to work around your attorney by direct negotiation with your spouse. Going behind his back undermines your position, however good your intentions. Well-meaning friends may tell you that a heart-to-heart talk with your wife may solve the division of property or another issue. Although this sounds good on the surface, if your relationship were good enough for honest and open negotiations, you probably wouldn't be getting divorced in the first place.

The other side of the coin is how to handle the situation if your spouse approaches you to discuss an aspect of the divorce. A request for an informal chat is like an invitation for a walk into a minefield. It is an effort to side-step the established channel of communication. You should always ask yourself; "What's in it for her?" because she's asking for her benefit, not yours. You might find yourself getting conned into making a concession with ramifications you don't fully understand. Without your attorney to advise you, you may lose your shirt. This is why you should always contact your attorney, before agreeing to any meeting.

Follow your attorney's advice and instructions. If there's something you don't understand, question him about it. After all, he's working for you, and you have a right to know why he wants to conduct a case in a certain way. However, never agree to do something he advises, and then go back on your word. You might be booby-trapping your entire effort. An example is if he tells you not to meet with your spouse, and not to return home for any reason. In some states, a separation agreement is null and void if the partners meet and have sex, for example. One act of passion can throw the entire case out the window. This is especially true in states which have divorce for cause, such as adultery. Your wife's attorney may, for example, use it to "prove" that you have forgiven her transgression.

Let's repeat to be sure: If your attorney asks you to do something and you don't understand why, don't ignore his advice. Instead, ask him why. It's his duty to explain it to you.

Always be open and candid with your attorney. If you feel that there are certain aspects of your relationship that he should not know, or if you don't feel that you can confide in him, you've got a real problem. Maybe you need to re-examine your motives, or maybe you need another attorney.

Remember the reason why lawyers are a cynical bunch: clients often lie to them. This is most true with criminal lawyers, but attorneys in other fields also find their clients deceptive. A husband may assure his attorney that he has not been having an affair, but this may be untrue. He may deny ever striking his wife, but three witnesses step forward to contradict him.

If you try to conceal your assets from the court, don't conceal them from your lawyer, too. A lawyer hates to be thought of as a liar, but he can appear to be one if his client hasn't been truthful with him and damaging facts come out in court. Your lawyer may be disturbed enough to withdraw from the case, and you really can't blame him. Nobody likes to be taken for a sucker.

Don't pull the rug out from under your lawyer in other ways, either. Don't, for example, threaten your wife in any way. With the current uproar over "domestic violence," any act that portrays you as aggressive or violent will play right into her hands. Another point to watch is harassment in any form. As we'll see, it's one thing to have the utilities cut off when you move, because this is often utility company policy when transferring service, but don't make the mistake of having service stopped once she gets it in her own name. Likewise with letters, telephone calls, and various forms of vandalism. If any such incidents occur, you can take it for granted that the court will believe her side of it, to your cost. You may get hit with an injunction, or a "peace bond," both of which can cost you time and money.

It's not enough to leave it all in the hands of your attorney. You have to take an active interest, because he has to be guided by your wishes. You also should know what is and isn't possible, in order not to have unrealistic expectations. Here are some questions for you and your attorney to discuss:

- How does the law in this state mandate property settlements?

- Is this a "community property" state?

Your attorney can inform you about the quirks in the community property law, which varies from state to state. It does not mean, as some assume, that all possessions are divided right down the middle. In some cases, only property acquired jointly during the marriage is "community property." Some states specifically exclude gifts. If you receive a gift from a relative, for example, and the gift is for you alone, it may not be part of the property settlement. Tools of your trade are automatically your property under California law, but not under Arizona's, or those of some other states. Another problem with community property is that if you own patents or copyrights which you earned during your marriage, the law gives your wife a share of any future royalties or payoffs.

- What about child custody?

Most states automatically award custody to the mother, but this is changing. In all states, there are provisions for awarding custody to the father, if the mother is "unfit." What constitutes "unfit," and how you prove it to the court, are the deciding factors.

- Do you want the children?

Do you really want to be responsible for their daily care, or do you only want to see them once a week? Keep in mind that, if you work, you'll have a hard time of it. You'll have to arrange for pre-school, or to take them to school, depending upon their ages. Ask yourself if you really want to be responsible for fixing their suppers, bathing them, and putting them to bed, after a hard day's work. If not, then, you should make it clear to your attorney that the children are only bargaining chips, to gain concessions from your wife.

- How does the law deal with alimony?

This can be crucial. Remember that many angry wives view alimony as a way of getting back at their husbands. Some want to make it difficult for their ex-husbands to resume dating, and feel that crippling him financially is the way to do it. In most cases, alimony depends on the wife's income and ability to work. The judge will also consider how long the couple has been married and how long the wife has been out of the job market.

- Does your wife have her own income?

Obviously, if she's got income, she needs less from you. If you've been married a short time, have no children, and earn about equal incomes, there may be no support payments at all.

- Financial Disclosure Statements.

These are statements, made under oath, listing your financial resources and debts. Typically, both husband and wife have to make them, unless they immediately agree regarding how to divide assets. Follow your lawyer's advice very carefully regarding these, and be sure of the information you provide under oath. An error can be used to hang you later. Likewise, alert your attorney to mis-statements you spot in your wife's affidavit. He can use these to destroy her credibility in court.

- Can she work?

Although your ex-wife may not be working at the moment, if she can work she will be able to support herself. Some wives have partial disabilities, which they exaggerate and exploit to obtain a free ride at their husband's expense. This is an especially nasty ploy, but the chances of success are in the wife's favor, even if she had worked before the marriage.

Judge-shopping

Among attorneys and others who spend much time in court, judges acquire reputations based upon their conduct in court and their decisions. Although many judges deny it, they often allow their prejudices to sway them in applying the law. The law may be clear in its meaning, but interpretation is another matter, and two judges can decide the same case quite differently. Some favor the wife regarding child custody, while others are noted for awarding huge support payments.

For your purposes, you need to appear before a judge who tends to treat husbands favorably. If your attorney is experienced in divorces, he'll know which judges are likely to decide for his clients. He may ask for a change of judge, unless he's concerned with his future appearances, as we've seen.

This can affect hearing scheduling. You may have to appear later than you'd expected, or at a time you feel is particularly inconvenient, to catch a particular judge. Discuss this with your attorney, and if he tells you that appearing before a certain judge will help your case, do all you can to work with him.

Negotiations

Chances are that your wife won't contest the separation itself, but the two issues which are almost always bitter are the property settlement and child custody. Although state law often lays out the basic principles, such as equal division of community property, there's always room for maneuver. Also remember that, although the court has the final say, the judge will expect you to have come to some sort of agreement before the hearing, so that he'll only have to resolve what you were unable to decide between yourselves.

It's important to agree to as much as possible before going into court. The reason is that informal negotiations cost relatively little, while a full-fledged court battle quickly becomes expensive. An obvious point is not to get involved in a knock-down, drag-out fight over something that's not worth it. It may be well worth it to "settle out of court," putting together an agreement that the judge needs only to scrutinize before rubber-stamping it. This is what's called a "default judgment."

Realistically, your wife is going to be angling for the best deal for herself, and if you don't understand what's happening, you can be losing instead of winning. At some point, you or your attorney will be negotiating with your wife or her attorney. It's better if you leave the negotiations to your attorney, for several reasons:

Objectivity

He can be more objective than you. In a face-to-face encounter, some of the things that led to the break-up of your relationship may get you angry, and if you're angry, you'll find thinking clearly difficult. Some wives use this against their husbands, and deliberately provoke them at meetings, to show that the husband has a hot temper or an unreasonable attitude.

Experience

You hired your attorney because he's a pro. He's been through this often, on behalf of many clients. He has the practice at conducting negotiations that you lack, unless you work as a negotiator yourself. He has seen the tricks and ploys, the hidden traps, and the other problems involved in negotiating divorce settlements. He's been faced with stances such as "What's mine is mine, and what's yours is negotiable," and knows how to handle them.

One way to describe negotiations is "positional bargaining." This means that both sides list their needs or demands, and trade off until both feel that they can live with the agreement. This is in sharp contrast to another school of thought, the "win-win" negotiation style. A win-win negotiator feels that the agreement should not only be fair, and agreeable to both sides, but should contain incentives for each side to maintain the agreement. This viewpoint is valid only when there's to be a continuing relationship. A divorce severs the relationship, and there's less need to retain good will. There are, however, two exceptions to this:

1. If there are children, you'll have to keep some form of communication open, unless you don't want to see your children again. If you have visitation rights, you'll need your ex-wife's cooperation to some extent. If she wants to, she can obstruct your visits, and you'll have a hard time of it.

2. Support payments of any sort depend entirely on your ability and willingness to pay. If your wife has an attorney, he'll be negligent if he fails to point out to her that payments that reduce you to poverty level may be impossible to collect. If they're so heavy that you can't live with them, you have no incentive to remain in the same position, and you may just as well quit your job, pull up stakes, and move elsewhere, leaving her with the problem of finding you and collecting. This is a very strong reason for not seeking punitive payments. Some wives, however, are so filled with hate that they can't understand this.

Apart from these exceptions, positional bargaining dominates divorce negotiations. Each side tries to work the best deal possible, without regard for the welfare of the other. It's definitely dog-eat-dog.

There are several important points to watch in positional bargaining:

- You know your wife best, and can advise your attorney regarding whether to take a "soft" or "hard" stance during negotiations. It's sometimes advisable not to risk antagonizing the other party, because this will simply increase resistance. On the other hand, if your wife thinks that being nice is being weak, you may as well go for broke. Being nice won't get you anything.

- Begin with a list of what you want, and rank the items in order of importance. You and your attorney should go over this list, but it's definitely not for the eyes of your wife or her lawyer.

- Don't be so anxious to get out of the relationship that you'll give away the whole store.

- Always ask for more than you need, or more than you expect to get. This is because it's easier to reduce your demands than to increase them. Remember that, if you don't do this, the other side will.

- Be prepared to make concessions. Negotiation is a process of "give and take." The art of trading off is making concessions that are less important to you to gain from the other side concessions that you value.

- Never give anything away. If the other side wants a concession, always ask for something in return.

- Be aware of what the other side really needs, and understand that there are some things that are not negotiable.

- Always ask for some things that you don't really want, to use as "bargaining chips" during negotiations.

- Always expect, and demand, a hard-and-fast commitment on each point. An example is visitation rights. Frequency and duration must be explicit, not described vaguely, in words such as "reasonable."

- If you concede child support payments, ask for an accounting in return. You have a right to know how your ex-wife is spending the money earmarked for the children. The law may not require such an accounting, but ask for it when negotiating the amount.

- Don't waste time arguing trivial points. Move on to something else if you can't reach agreement immediately, and return later.

- Don't let the other side dictate the scope and pace of the negotiations. The other attorney may want to straight-jacket you by slipping in some rules such as "Let's decide on the division of estate before we get on to alimony," or some such. Don't agree to anything like this. Insist upon your freedom to trade back and forth, instead of being backed into a corner.

- Finally, always get it in writing. Always. A verbal agreement means nothing. It may be legally binding, according to statute, but proving it may be impossible if the other party denies having made it. Any promises or concessions the other party offers verbally should receive only one answer from your side: "Are you willing to put that in writing?"

Courtroom Demeanor

What happens in court in real life is very unlike what you see on TV, and you'd better be prepared for it. As a start, you can expect much less emotional intensity, because real-life lawyers, judges, and court officers do this every day, and frankly, it gets old. If it's an uncontested divorce with no disagreement over property or children, the proceedings may bore you tremendously, because little seems to be happening.

There are several basic points to understand about court appearances. First, you do have the choice of being represented by a lawyer or not. If you have hired a lawyer, leave the driving to him during the court session. If you think he's mis-managing your case, don't get into a long discussion with him inside the court. Do it outside, and if you're truly dissatisfied, get another lawyer.

If you choose to represent yourself, you can expect the court to be half-way on your side. The reason is that, as a lay person, you do not know the ins and outs of court procedure, and are unfamiliar with the motions you can make to the court. A "motion" is a request for a ruling or a decision, and the court may grant it or not. If you're representing yourself, the court will routinely make the appropriate motions for you, so that the record shows that you got a "fair" hearing. Whether it's fair or not depends a lot upon the judge.

Dress appropriately, but not expensively. If you look like a millionaire, you can expect the judge to be influenced by your apparent wealth, and sock it to you in proportion.

You need emotional control during a court session. If you can "deadpan" everything, so much the better. If you become excited, and it shows, it will count against you, especially if your wife has accused you of physical or emotional brutality. The most important reason, though, is to avoid antagonizing the judge. In court, you're on the judge's turf, and you have to act by the judge's rules. If you disagree with anything said, let your lawyer make any appropriate objections. Do not comment or sneer at anything you hear, even if your wife is on the stand lying through her teeth. Always remember, decorum counts more than being right in court, no matter what any lawyer or judge may tell you.

Judges are human, too, and are just as vulnerable to first impressions and subliminal cues as the rest of us. If your wife can put across the image of a vulnerable creature who has been terribly wronged by a monster of a husband, it can influence the judge. If a judge starts to dislike you, because you're speaking out of turn or not showing appropriate respect, it will influence his decision.

You can expect the judge to announce the decision in several parts. The routine part will be the granting of the divorce decree. Another is the immediate property settlement. The question of support payments is another part, as is the issue of child custody. Don't expect all of these to be in your favor. It might work out that most are against you.

If this happens, say nothing. Even if you feel a blind rage at how your wife, with the aid of the court, has trampled your rights and taken you to the cleaners, hold your tongue. Play it cool, because while you're in court, you're most vulnerable. If you lose self-control, you may not walk out of court a free man. The judge can have you jailed, without trial, for "contempt of court." Better believe it.

Sit down, keep your mouth shut, and begin planning whether or not you can live with the court's judgment. If you can't, understand that your chances of getting anything with an appeal are poor. Your only chance is to skip out, taking whatever assets you can with you.

Answering specific questions in court may be difficult or painful. However, the process is the same as with an interrogatory, which we'll discuss later. We'll delve into techniques of handling questions at that point.

Blackmail

This is a nasty word, but it's an accurate description of what happens during some divorce negotiations. If you've got a guilty little secret which your wife has discovered, two things can happen: She may use this against you in a spirit of malice, to ruin your reputation or your business, or she may use it in a more calculating way, to get what she wants from you. If this is the case, she or her attorney will make you "an offer you can't refuse."

Negotiation works only if both parties begin as approximate equals. If, on the other hand, one party holds all the cards, it's no longer negotiation; it's an ultimatum. A few examples will show the point:

Adultery is so common that it's conditionally accepted in most American communities today. At least, it doesn't wreck a person's life if it comes to light. However, if you're a clergyman who's been getting a little sex on the side, you'll find it very traumatic to have evidence of your hobby revealed. If you live in one of the few states in which divorce on grounds is still the law, adultery can saddle you with a heavy burden, and your ex-wife-to-be may use this to wring painful concessions from you. This is especially true if adultery is a felony. Although this sort of law is rarely enforced, yours might be one of the rare cases.

If you're into an illegal activity, the threat of sending evidence to the appropriate enforcement authorities will get your attention. You'll then be faced with a hard choice.

Your attorney will probably advise you to fold your hand and concede whatever your wife wishes. Giving her the house, the car, and the children, beats going to prison for several years, or losing your livelihood if you're in a sensitive occupation. In one sense, you're getting off cheaply.

This is why you must be discreet in your peccadilloes, and frank with your attorney. If you have any inkling that your ex-wife-to-be may have a nasty surprise in store for you, tell him about it. He may have a bright idea regarding how to work around it. If, instead, you let it come as a surprise to him, it'll be a no-win situation.

The other side of the coin is legal harassment. Your attorney may ask you if your wife has any flaws he might exploit. Even if she does not, he may advise tactics such as issuing subpoenas for depositions to her friends, employer, and fellow workers, and questioning them about her morals and personal habits. Adroit questioning can give witnesses the impression that the attorney is really onto something, and cause her embarrassment.

Legal Harassment

If one party is nasty or vindictive, there are ways to cause headaches for the other by using the law and legal stratagems. It's particularly attractive for the wife if she knows that her husband will have to pay attorney's fees for both sides. She can then take him over the bumps at his expense, all the way. Let's look at some of the specific harassment methods:

Interrogatories

A simple way is to claim that the husband has hidden assets, or that he's been secretive about his finances. If your wife makes this statement to her attorney, he can have you fill out a long and detailed questionnaire, known in the trade as an "interrogatory." You're obliged to answer in writing, under oath.

Interrogatories basically cover your life history, including name, place of birth, date of birth, social security number, dates and places of all marriages, and divorces. They also cover your present address, the names and relationships of anyone living with you, when you moved there, and how much rent you pay.

Your criminal record, if any, will also be the subject of questions. So will your employment history, and you'll be required to list all employment you held during the term of your marriage, including company name, address, name of supervisor, dates employed, type of work performed, pay rate, overtime, and net income. This will include part-time work.

If you're working under contract, you'll also have to furnish information about the terms of each written agreement, including the name and address of each party to the agreement, terms of the agreement, name and address of each person who has a copy of the agreement, and you'll also have to attach a copy of each agreement to the interrogatory.

You'll also have to include information about all tax returns filed since the date of your marriage, including whether it was separate or joint, the year for which it was filed, the income figures, the source of income, the name and address of the person who prepared each return, and the name and address of anyone who has a copy of the return.

You'll also have to include a current financial statement, including your gross and take-home pay, deductions for federal and state income taxes, FICA, state disability premiums, insurance premiums, retirement contributions, union dues, credit union payments, wage assessments, charitable contributions, savings plans, employee welfare fund, and any other deductions.

If you're compensated on the basis of commission, you'll have to answer a plethora of nit-picking questions about every detail of your earnings, including draws and dates on which you collect, method of computation, whether commissions are payable prior to delivery and acceptance of merchandise sold, and charge-backs, if any.

Any other type of compensation also comes under scrutiny, and you'll have to furnish details of any you receive, which can include:

- Living Accommodations
- Meals
- Discounts on merchandise and transportation
- Uniforms or clothing

- Medical services
- Credit cards

You'll have to list your educational accomplishments, including names and addresses of schools, dates attended, courses of study, and degrees.

If you've had any personal financial statements of any kind prepared during your marriage, you'll have to furnish detailed information on each one.

If you've been a partner in any business, you'll have to furnish complete information on each business, including name and address, type of business, names and addresses of partners, dates the business started and when you acquired your interest, present value of your interest, your percentage interest, and other information. Likewise if you have owned any shares of stock during your marriage.

You'll also have to list all of your assets, including all furniture and household goods, dates purchased, price paid, source of funds used to buy each piece, present value, etc.

Another category is savings and checking accounts, money market accounts, certificates of deposit, in your name alone or with others. This includes all you've had during your marriage, and the details you'll have to furnish are name and address of bank, type of account, account number, owners' names appearing on the account, persons authorized to sign on the account, date opened, date closed, if applicable, and present balance, if applicable. You'll also be asked to give similar information on any accounts on which your name did not appear, if you deposited any money into them or withdrew money from them.

You'll have to list any safe deposit boxes or vaults into which you deposited money, valuables, or other items of personal property during your marriage. Information will cover name, place, dates started, dates ended, and the use to which you put each one.

If you own interest in any patent or copyright, you'll have to list each one, in nit-picking detail.

If you have any debts or outstanding obligations, including mortgages, conditional sales, etc., you'll have to provide similar information for each. This also includes credit card accounts, charge accounts, etc. You'll also have to list all credit cards which you've used, for any reason, during the previous year.

If any person or corporation owes you money, you'll have to list them, providing similar details. Likewise any tax liabilities you may owe.

If you own a car, you'll have to provide the make, year, model, and license number, the name of the legal owner, registered owner, the purchase date and price, name and address of dealer, and the name and address of each person who has made payments on the car.

You'll also have to provide detailed information on any other personal property you own, as well as any real estate you own or may have owned during the time of your marriage. This will include property improvements.

You'll also find a question regarding any gifts to relatives, friends, or anyone else. Gifts may be money, or other things of value. If you've made any, you'll have to list the name and address of each recipient, relationship to you, value of each gift, date given, and the reason for each one. Likewise for any you've received during your marriage.

Trusts and inheritances are also covered in great detail, including those you may have received, and any you've created.

You'll also have to list, in great detail, any insurance policies of any sort you hold, or held during the course of your present marriage. This includes privately-purchased insurance policies, and those you have as part of your employment.

Financial records are also part of the picture, and you'll have to list all that you have, including bank statements, canceled checks, etc.

Retirement income plans, profit sharing plans, pension funds, etc., are also among the assets you'll have to list. You'll have to list the date acquired, the nature and extent of your rights, what portion is vested and what portion is not, names and addresses of parties from whom acquired, and other details.

Membership in any club, organization, or association must also be listed, if you pay any dues or regular charges. As with other categories, you'll have to list name, address, date membership started, the nature of your participation in each organization, and the monthly amount you pay.

Another category is listing disabilities, physical and mental. This includes names and addresses of doctors who have diagnosed or treated each disability.

Pre-nuptial agreements, as well as any other agreements relating to rights and interests to property, are also covered. You'll have to list each agreement, including date, reasons for each agreement, description of property covered, amendments to the agreement, and the details of each change.

You'll also have to list the names and addresses of any people who have knowledge of any facts involved in the dispute, any witnesses you intend to call, any documents you intend to introduce as evidence, and copies of any written statements you intend to introduce as evidence.

In states in which divorce is "for cause," you may also have to answer whether you ever made statements such as the following:

- That you did not love your spouse.

- That you were dissatisfied sexually with your spouse.

- That you were dissatisfied with her as an intellectual companion, parent, or housekeeper.

- Dissatisfaction regarding her manner of speech, dress, and family background are also included.

- That you stated that your marriage was a mistake.

For each, you'll have to list the reason for the statement, how many times made, to whom, and the names and addresses of any persons who heard the statement.

Filling out such an interrogatory can be a back-breaking chore, if you let it be. If you're lucky enough not to have many business interests, it will be easier, because you can go down several pages writing "N/A" to questions relating to partnerships and corporations. In other cases, the answers to questions will be in documents in your wife's possession. This lets you off the hook.

Consult with your lawyer before beginning to answer the questions. He may be able to find solid grounds to objecting to some of the questions. Going over the interrogatory with him may disclose many areas which you may ignore, and reduce your workload.

Inspection Orders

Another way to harass you is to obtain an order for you to deliver to her attorney your financial records, including your savings book, checkbook, credit cards, and safe deposit box key, for "inspection." Before you agree to such a move, make sure you know exactly the terms and conditions of the "inspection." One trick is to set a time of 5 P.M., which just by coincidence happens to be closing time for many offices. You arrive with your box full of papers, and the secretary tells you that the attorney has already left for the day, and to leave the material with her. If you agree to this, they've GOTCHA. You may return the next day, to be told that your papers, including your checkbook and credit cards, have been moved to another office, or that the attorney hasn't told the secretary where he was going, etc. Granted, the material is yours, but effectively, you are prevented from access to it. Possession is nine-tenths of the law, and getting it back can be a hassle. This is why you must "think paranoid" if such a prospect arises.

One solution to this problem is to furnish only photocopies. Check with your attorney on this, as you may be able to avoid turning over any originals.

Depositions

These are question-and-answer sessions, taken under oath. Your wife's attorney will ask you questions, and you are required to answer. Generally, you're allowed to have your attorney present, and you should do so. Your wife's lawyer is less likely to try to bulldoze you than he might be if you were facing him alone. Your attorney knows the law better than you do, and he can object to certain questions, knowing that he's right.

When responding to questions, listen carefully, and pause before answering. Look at him while speaking. Have your answer well thought-out, and give your attorney time to object, if appropriate. If he doesn't raise any objection, you must answer the question. In doing so, don't guess. Be sure of your answer before you open your mouth, and don't be afraid to say "I don't know," or "I don't remember." However, don't overdo it. Provide any information which you reasonably should know. A series of "I don't know" responses doesn't look good, and if you try this when you get to court, the judge will whack you for it.

Another important point is never to volunteer information. Answer only the question asked. Don't anticipate his next question and give him a freebie. Make him work for his money. If you give him a piece of information he didn't have, it can easily lead to another series of questions, possibly exploring an area you'd rather not have probed.

Conventional wisdom about lawyers is that they never ask a question unless they already know the answer. Not so. Lawyers don't always know the answers before they ask their questions, and understanding this can save you a lot of anxiety. Some questions are pure boilerplate, and the lawyer knows that they don't really apply to you, but asks them just to cover his bases. He also knows that, if he asks his questions in a confident, authoritative manner, he'll psych out some people and bluff them into thinking that he knows something he really doesn't.

This is why it's worth practicing dead-panning your answers. Learn self-control, to avoid showing surprise or discomfort at any questions. Her attorney will be watching you carefully, and looking for signs of distress to reveal sensitive areas. This is why your manner mustn't give him any clues.

You may be surprised to find that some of his questions reveal things you never knew. If, for example, he asks when you discovered your wife's affair with another man, and you didn't know about it, he's just let slip a freebie.

You may also be surprised to find that the rules somehow don't seem to apply equally during a deposition hearing. Your wife's attorney may inform you that you must be truthful, under penalty of perjury, but your wife may lie like hell. The reason is that these are merely intimidation tactics. It very rarely happens that a spouse actually faces prosecution for perjury. This is why you mustn't let your wife's attorney psych you out. Lie, if you think you can get away with it, because she will.

Show Cause Orders

Your wife's attorney will almost surely go for a "show cause" order, to get a judge to award your wife temporary support. This is normal, but it can sometimes be zany.

In one spectacular case, a temporary settlement awarded the wife of Jean Laurent Andreani $40,000 per month in alimony and $7,500 per month in child support. Andreani is a millionaire who owns a lot of income-producing real estate in Maricopa County, Arizona, and Commissioner John Trombino, of the Maricopa County Superior Court, decided that he was fully able to support his wife and children in an opulent lifestyle. His wife got the house, the Rolls-Royce, and the Mercedes 560. Trombino also ordered Andreani to pay his wife's $100,000 legal bill, and pay for his children's private school tuition.[2]

A show cause order can turn into legal harassment, though. Your wife's attorney may claim that you have been somehow irresponsible with the family finances, or have left your wife penniless, and obtain a court order for you to deliver all of your money to the court or to her, for "safekeeping."

The petition usually states that your wife doesn't have enough money on which to live, no means of support, and that you took all of the money with you. The critical phrasing usually goes like this:

"That (your name) should be ordered to deliver the community savings, and any other liquid assets of the community into the possession of the court, or into the care of (her name) for safekeeping until such time as the court has made a determination as to the final distribution of these assets."

The petition may also request the court to order you to pay her attorney's fees, simply because this is a convenient place to request it. If followed literally, this strips you of every cent, including the cash in your pockets. The trap is that, if you fail to show for the hearing, the judge may issue a civil warrant for your arrest.

It appears frightening on the surface, but don't let it worry you too much. In practice, lawyers ask for the whole world, as a negotiating tactic, figuring that they can always back down, but that if they don't ask in the first place, they won't get it. Judges know this, and they usually award what they feel is right, regardless of an attorney's posturing.

Sources

1. *Discretionary Justice*, Howard Abadinsky, Springfield, IL, Charles C. Thomas, Publisher, 1984, pp. 69-74.

2. *Arizona Republic*, March 18, 1990.

9

Take The Money
And Run

Controlling the money is a major part of controlling the relationship. The partner with ready cash has the freedom to pull
up stakes and leave at will. Likewise, anyone with a credit card
can rent a car, buy airline tickets, and even pay for a cruise, at
the expense of the person who pays the bills on the account.

We've already made the point that family finances ought to
be under your control. This isn't always possible. Your wife may
not like having you hold all of the purse-strings. How you handle
this depends on your situation, and your persuasiveness.

Who Earns the Bread?

The first point is that, if you're the breadwinner, you're
unquestionably in the driver's seat. You earn the money, and
you disburse it as you see fit. This doesn't mean that you have

to adopt a dictatorial manner, but simply retain the final say. You may allow your wife a certain sum to buy food, and pay other bills. You may even establish a separate credit card account for her, if she feels she needs one. However, be careful with credit cards!

Credit Card Hazards

Having her credit card on a separate account from yours allows you better control, because you can set the limit. You may have a VISA card with a $5,000 limit, but the account you set up for her may have a limit of only $200 or $500. You should make certain, when you set up the account with the bank, that the limit will remain fixed. This is important, because credit card issuers often implement automatic increases for accounts with good credit records. This is simply an effort to encourage you to run up larger debts, so that they can earn more interest. If this happens, the account you set up with an original $500 limit, for example, can grow to have a $5,000 limit, without your knowledge. This is dangerous, and you need to avoid this like the plague!

The second case to consider is your wife's having her own income. If you both work, it's almost certain she won't meekly hand over her paycheck to you, but will want to prove her "independence" by having at least a joint account. She may even want a separate account. Legally, she can open one without your permission, or even knowledge.

There are pros and cons to joint and separate accounts. You also ought to know how joint accounts work, and how each type has advantages and disadvantages. A checking account, for example, can be set up as "John and Mary Smith," or "John or Mary Smith." The first type, with an "and" between the names, requires both signatures on each check. This can be cumbersome, but it ensures that neither can write a check without the consent and active participation of the other. The second type requires only one signature. This is more convenient for routine transactions, but it also means that either party can withdraw the balance at any time.

Separate accounts are preferable. An "or" type joint account, unless you keep the balance low enough to meet only immediate needs, gives her an opportunity to loot your finances. This is especially true if a plastic card goes with the account. A VISA or Mastercard introduces a line of credit that may be very high. A check guarantee card allows your wife to overdraw the account, another possible source of trouble.

This leads us to another problem: who pays the debts? If yours is a typical American family, you're several thousands of dollars in debt. At the very least, you pay federal, state, and local governments thousands of dollars in taxes each year. A basic mistake some men make is to pay the entire tax burden themselves, even if the wife has her own income. This sort of gentlemanly behavior allows your wife to loot your finances in a low-grade, low-key manner. Why should you pay her taxes?

It's a basic mistake to allow your wife to enjoy her own income, and spend it on what she wishes, while you suffer the burden of paying all of the bills. This can lead to serious abuses, and even to her building up a bug-out fund to sustain her in case she ever decides to leave you. If she has an out-of-state bank account, this is very likely.

Calculating Your Income

This is easy if you earn a salary. If, on the other hand, you're self-employed or you have several sources of income, it can be a ball of wax. It's unfortunate, but true, that many men don't know exactly how much they really earn.

The figure your wife will be scrutinizing, in anticipating the amount of support payments she'll receive, is your gross income. What's really relevant is your net income, after expenses and after taxes. The reason is obvious, as even the most incompetent attorney can point out to her:

If you're self-employed, and gross one million dollars a year, but have to spend $960,000 for expenses, your real income is only $40,000. This can easily happen if you're in a wholesale or retail business, and most of the cash flow relates to movement of stock. You buy $960,000 worth of material, and re-sell it for one million dollars. Any judge who awarded her half a million dollars a year in support payments would accomplish only one thing: He'd guarantee that she would collect only the first payment, at most, because your business would sink immediately.

Calculating your real income may require an accountant, if you have a mixture of commissions, profits, stock and bond dividends, and interest income. If it's so complex that you can't make a good estimate, you'd better leave it to a pro. Another reason is that, even though accountants often play fast and loose with the figures to suit their clients' needs, a judge will still accept an accountant's figures as less biased than yours.

Calculating Debts

If you owe a lot of money, it can cause quite a problem in the property settlement. Fortunately, the problem may kick back at your wife more than it does at you. Let's see how your debts stack up, and how they affect the property settlement. Begin by listing and estimating the value of your assets using the following forms.

Asset Inventory and Valuation

Asset Description   **Cash Value**

Real Estate:

  Main Residence   _____

  Vacation Property   _____

  Other Real Estate:

  _____   _____

  _____   _____

Vehicles:

  Automobile #1   _____

  Automobile #2   _____

  Other Vehicles (Cars, Motorcycles, Boats):

  _____   _____

  _____   _____

  _____   _____

Major Appliances:

  _____   _____

  _____   _____

  _____   _____

Jewelry and Furs:

  Yours   _____

  Your Wife's   _____

Asset Inventory and Valuation
(Continued)

Asset Description   **Cash Value**

Electronic Equipment:
   Television   _____
   VCR   _____
   CamCorder   _____
   Video Game Unit   _____
   Stereo Equipment   _____
   Photographic Equipment   _____
   Computer & Accessories   _____
   Other Electronic Equipment:

   _____   _____
   _____   _____

Tools:

   Power Tools (Saws, Drills, Air Compressor, Cranes, Shop Vacuum, etc.)

   _____   _____
   _____   _____
   _____   _____

   Hand Tools   _____

   Garden Tools (Lawnmower, Ladders, Rakes, etc.)

   _____   _____
   _____   _____

Sporting Goods: (Golf Clubs, Skis, Bicycles, etc.)

   _____   _____
   _____   _____

Other Personal Property: (Books, Clothing, Rugs, Artwork, etc.)

   _____   _____
   _____   _____

Asset Inventory and Valuation
(Continued)

Asset Description   **Cash Value**

Furniture:

  Bedroom #1 (Beds, Dressers, Tables, Lamps):

    _____   _____

    _____   _____

  Bedroom #2 (Beds, Dressers, Tables, Lamps):

    _____   _____

    _____   _____

  Bedroom #3 (Beds, Dressers, Tables, Lamps):

    _____   _____

    _____   _____

  Living Room (Sofa, Chairs, Tables, Lamps):

    _____   _____

    _____   _____

  Dining Room (Table, Chairs, Bureau, Cabinets):

    _____   _____

    _____   _____

  Kitchen (Silverware, Dishes, Pots & Pans, Bowls):

    _____   _____

    _____   _____

  Other Furniture:

    _____   _____

Now list your debts using the following liabilities form.

Liabilities

Source of Debt   **Current Balance**

Real Estate Loans (Mortgages, Contracts, etc.):

  Main Residence _____   _____

  Other Real Estate:

  _____   _____

  _____   _____

Home Equity Loans:

_____   _____

_____   _____

_____   _____

Auto and Boat Loans:

_____   _____

_____   _____

_____   _____

Credit Cards (VISA, MasterCard, Gasoline, Store Cards, etc.):

_____   _____

_____   _____

_____   _____

_____   _____

_____   _____

Any Other Debts:

_____   _____

_____   _____

_____   _____

Which is larger? Subtract the smaller figure from the larger one, to find your "net worth." This is the net value of your assets, or debts. If you owe more than you own, you have a negative net worth. This reduces the slice of the pie each gets, because part of your future income is already committed to pay off the debts. If your assets, on the other hand, exceed the total of your debts, you have a positive net worth, and this is gravy. Unfortunately, it's gravy for everybody, and your wife will expect a bigger slice of the pie. It also means that both attorneys will be more liberal in spending time (which is money) on the case.

Traditionally, the husband is responsible for the debts. This is, however, a gray area. If you have an income and your wife does not, you're stuck with the debts, like it or not. In a community property state, where your joint ownings get divided down the middle, so do the debts, and the court will most likely rule that they get paid from your joint assets before the final split. An exception is a house mortgage, which can easily have an outstanding principal exceeding your joint assets. In any case, state laws and individual cases vary, so go by your lawyer's advice.

Another nasty aspect of a divorce's financial settlement is that, if you have to sell your house, you'll have to pay capital gains tax on the amount it's appreciated. This, combined with the real estate agent's commission, and the closing costs, means that you'll take a bath in the end. One way to avoid this is to have your wife take the house as part of her settlement. If you own your own business, this makes sense, especially if your wife can't run the business. You can always buy another house.

Financial Records

Another point to watch is keeping financial records under your control. If you're ever faced with an injunction, covered in a later chapter, take your financial records with you. Also remember that, if your wife obtains an injunction against you, she may already have hidden the records, so retain control of them, always. Depriving your wife of the paperwork denies her the opportunity to get you into trouble with the tax man, or to document your income. If she or her attorney want something, let them work for it. Don't give anything away without a court order.

The other side of the coin is to make sure to have your lawyer subpoena your wife's financial records. This is especially true if she does not work, and gives a "Who, me?" response to questions regarding any bank accounts she may have.

Avoiding Dangers

There are a couple of booby-traps for the unwary. Some try to conceal assets in various ways. One is withdrawing cash and hiding it in a safe deposit box, or burying it in the yard. Another is transferring assets to friends and relatives, creating bills of sale for nominal sums, in an effort to reduce the estate that will be divided. Another, for the man who owns his own business, is to invest most of his cash into the business in order to reduce the amount available for splitting with his ex-wife. Such tricks are cute, but lawyers and judges know them all. Try them, and they'll cut you off at the knees. Another problem is playing games with the IRS. They scrutinize divorce proceedings because they know that some people play such games, and they're experts at uncovering them.

The hard fact is that, if you're going to conceal assets and play other fiscal games, the time to start is long before you're thinking of divorce. The underground economy is alive and well in America, and it's also very profitable. You do have to get into it early, and you must keep it a secret. What your wife doesn't know can't hurt you.

Reducing Your Income

If you can reduce your income, you'll offer less for your wife and her lawyer to bite off. However, this is something you have to begin very early. You can't quit your job the day after you or your wife files for divorce, because that's too blatant. The court won't buy it, and you're better off not doing this unless you intend to leave the state.

You have to begin at least a year in advance, because you'll probably have to file an affidavit listing your income and expenses for the previous year, to establish a baseline for support payments. Ideally, you should be able to show that your wife earns more than you, but realistically, this isn't likely to happen.

If you're self-employed, you'll find it easier to reduce your income than if you're a wage slave. The simplest way is to stop seeking new business, because existing accounts tend to die at an average rate of 10% per year, and you'll find that this attrition, coupled with inflation, will make a healthy dent in your income.

Another way, again available to you only if you're self-employed, is to reduce your net income by increasing your business's expenses. This is something you have to begin doing well before the divorce, to avoid making it obvious.

A sore point is income from patents, royalties, and residuals, which are payments made long after you've actually performed the work. In the "Garrett" case, Garrett's wife was able to claim part of her husband's future income, because as an attorney, he'd taken on some contingency-fee cases, and payments continued long after he'd performed the bulk of the work.

Make no mistake; you can get screwed royally on this one. The only way to avoid this fearful prospect is to take action early. Sell your interests for cash before you file for divorce, and spend the proceeds on something for yourself. In selling now, you'll never collect 100% of what your patents or residuals are worth, but you'll prevent your wife from bleeding your future income.

These steps are important, because they will have an impact on both the property settlement and another factor which can affect you for years: support payments.

Support Payments

Whether classed as alimony or child support, payments stretching into the indefinite future form a chain around your neck. Having your future earnings spent before you earn them is a painful way to live. However, there are some gray areas, and some ways to obtain concessions and reductions. Let's look at several typical cases:

- You're married less than a year, with no children, and both you and your wife work, earning about equal incomes. The odds are that there will be no alimony, and of course, no child support.

- You've been married ten years, to a woman who has never worked, and has no marketable skills. You earn enough to support both of you separately. Chances are that you'll have to pay alimony until she re-marries. Better hope that she does.

- Same as above, but your wife has a physical ailment, such as multiple sclerosis, making her incapable of working. You'll have to support her for the rest of her life, as her chances of re-marrying are poor.

- Same as above, but you have three children. You'll have to pay both alimony and child support payments.

- Same as the second case, but your ex-wife remarries six months after the divorce. The alimony stops right then.

One point you'd better understand clearly is that modern feminists feel that, although the wife has earned less than the husband, or even nothing at all during their marriage, she's fully entitled to a major share of his assets. One women's advocate states boldly that "her contributions and her worth are so vast that they can't even be calculated."[1] She goes on to make the blanket assumption that without the wife, the husband would not be where he is today. She does not even mention the value of the husband, when he takes on the roles of plumber, painter, auto mechanic, electrician, appliance repairman, taxi driver, gardener, etc. With this viewpoint, the wife can easily feel justified to rape the husband's assets, and feel that she's being merciful because she's not having him castrated or killed.

This is an example of the "gold mine" school of thought, common among angry wives and greedy divorce lawyers: the wife gets the gold, and the husband gets the shaft.

State laws vary regarding how to compute alimony and child support payments. They also vary regarding whether or not the biological father has to provide child support after the mother remarries.

Support payments may not appear to be much, but they add up to a grand sum over the years. Let's hypothesize that you're ordered to pay $400 per month. In one year, that comes to $4,800, and over ten years, it totals $48,000.

It's in your interest to try for minimal support payments, or to wring concessions in return for such payments. The drawback is that your wife can later ask the court for higher payments on the grounds of inflation and higher cost of living. If your income rises, she can also ask the court for a proportional increase in her payments. Of course, if your income drops, you can ask the court for a reduction, but your chances of getting it are poor.

Another way to do it is to offer a larger slice of the immediate property in return for a limitation or elimination of future payments. The advantage this offers you is that this eliminates the hold she has on your future income. This may be hard to take, at first, but it can be a bargain, especially if you anticipate earning substantially more in the future than you do now. It takes guts to make such a decision, because the reward for you is both uncertain and delayed.

Let's also look at the other side of the coin. What if you anticipate your income dropping over the next ten or twenty years? This can happen. You may be employed in a dying field. Buggy whip manufacturing was once a solid industry in this country. So was the manufacture of slide rules. Civilian electronic goods, such as stereos and VCRs, are increasingly made in other countries. If you're in a dying field, you may be unemployed or on skid row in ten years. If this is your future, take what you can now, and promise her anything for later.

Decreeing support payments is one thing. Enforcing the decree is another. There are occasional outcries over child support deadbeats, and occasionally, some of them go to jail. The fact remains, however, that these are civil, and not criminal matters. Police agencies and sheriff's departments are overloaded with warrants for criminal cases, such as parole violations, which is why civil cases take very low priority. Practically nobody goes to jail for missing alimony payments.

The good news is that alimony is tax-deductible on the federal return. The bad news is that lump-sum cash or property settlements, voluntary payments not made under a court order or a written separation agreement, or child support, are not. To spare you a world of hurt on taxes, the ideal would be a court order mandating a property settlement to be paid as a series of large alimony payments spread over a year. In practice, your wife's attorney won't be so solicitous of sparing you the tax burden as to agree to this. The judge, too, is unlikely to care.

Your wife may, to be spiteful, ask her lawyer to push for large child support payments and small alimony. This gives you the worst possible tax picture, because you won't be able to deduct much.

Your ex-wife will have to declare alimony payments as income, and she will have to pay tax on them. She does not have to report child support payments. You can, under certain conditions, claim your children as dependents.

The main point of this section is that, if you can obtain a "walk away" deal, with no support payments, it's worth it. You may have to hand over a lot of cash or property to get your wife to relinquish claims on your future income, but it's usually worth it.

Will You Need An Accountant?

The answer depends on how complicated your financial status is. If your income is from wages, and you and your wife own a small amount of personal and real property, it should be fairly easy to add up your assets, subtract your debts, and come up with a net worth. You may already have done so, using the worksheets provided starting on page 123.

If you own part or all of a business, and there's a complicated network of financial entanglements, it may take a CPA to sort it all out. You may need an appraiser to estimate the value of property you own, and this offers some latitude for valuing your property high or low.

The final answer is how much you think you're worth, and stand to lose, in relation to the cost of the accountant's time. Remember that some attorneys are buddy-buddy with accountants, and they specialize in referring clients to one another. Unless you stand to lose more than the accountant will charge you, it's not worth the trouble.

Financial Misconduct

This affects the property settlement in some states. The party who can show that the other one has done some sneaky things with the family finances can score points with the court. One obvious example is the wife's running up a credit card account after separation. It's self-evident that this is vengeful, and the court will take it into account. Even if the law does not provide specifically for consideration of financial shenanigans, the judge may be swayed by the facts in rendering his judgment.

In some circumstances, you can seize some of the assets and make it look like "self-defense." If, for example, you have paperwork to prove that your wife was giving away large sums of your money to her friends, or spending it on vacations, without your knowledge, you can show this to be cause for concern, and convince a court that you closed out all of the accounts to prevent her wasting the rest.

To make this work, you need two things. The first is paperwork to show that your wife was exercising bad faith. If, for example, you find a wad of money order receipts, for payments about which she'd told you nothing, this is documentary evidence. This is especially true if you had joint checking and credit card accounts. It will be very difficult for her to explain why she found it necessary to pay via money order. It will look as if she was "laundering" her payments to keep you from finding out about them.

The second point is what you do with the assets you take over. If you simply put them in an account, such as a money market or certificate of deposit, and spend only what you need for legitimate expenses, you'll be showing that you're acting responsibly. This will score points for you in court.

Financial Disclosures

One aspect of deciding on a financial settlement is that your wife, her lawyer, and the court will want to know details of your financial affairs that you may have thought were private. Forget it! They'll ask for the information, and you won't have the right to refuse. One way is to obtain documents from you by subpoena. Let's look at some of the things they may request:

- Copies of your income tax returns for the last three or five years.
- Lists of any investments.
- Lists of any insurance policies.
- Lists of any and all bank accounts in your name.
- Any pension or profit-sharing plan you have with your employer.

Another way of obtaining information is to present you with an "interrogatory," a set of written questions. You must answer them under oath. The third way is by a deposition, which as we've seen, is a session during which her lawyer questions you under oath.[2]

You can be certain that your wife and her lawyer will pore over this information, seeking the best way to strip you bare. One way is to seek a cash settlement, instead of property. The reason? She doesn't want to be saddled with investment properties, for example, which require a cash outlay in taxes for upkeep. She also may not want the house, if you have one, because maintenance and taxes can be a drain on her finances. She'd rather take the money and run, leaving you stuck with the obligations.[3]

Tip! If your wife and her lawyer make you a first offer of keeping the property, you'd better look for undisclosed assets.

She has to have front money for the lawyer, and operating capital to pay taxes and upkeep on the house or whatever property she wants. She may have a secret bank account or two to tide her over the difficult period. Find it, and you can undermine her case.

Economic Warfare

You have to deal with this topic, because you can't avoid making certain decisions which will affect both your plans. When you decide to break up, almost anything you do will affect your wife's ability to survive economically. In some cases, simply moving out will force certain responsibilities upon her. You can also take certain steps to cripple her finances, which may be desirable from a tactical point of view.

You will, of course, have your own attorney. Whether your wife also has one to look after her interests depends mostly on whether she has the front money to hire one. Many divorce attorneys want money up front, and this starts at about a thousand dollars. If she's scraping just to pay the rent, or put food on the table, she won't be able to hire an attorney. The exceptions are if there's a "Legal Aid Society" in your locale, or if she has an attorney as a relative or friend.

As we've seen, you will probably be required to attend a "show cause" hearing, in which you will have to show cause why you should not make support payments to her during the divorce proceedings. Your wife will be pleading poverty and asking the judge to order you to support her in the style to which she has become accustomed. This is one way vengeful wives have of hurting the husband, because support payments allow them to take their time in litigation.

Another trick wives pull to obtain legal aid and handicap their husbands is to ask the court to make husbands pay their legal fees, too. This really puts pressure on the husband, because he now has to pay for both, and if the wife chooses to spin out the proceedings, she can really stick it to him.

There are several steps you can take to put economic pressure upon her. For maximum effect, don't wait until legal proceedings are starting. The earlier you begin, the more effective your defensive steps will be, and there won't be any injunctions to cramp your style. Start before the break-up, and cover these points:

■ Begin by cleaning out the credit card and bank accounts. This is defensive, to prevent her from taking the money and running, but also strips her liquid assets. It's less important if you jointly own stocks, which are not as handy as cash or credit cards.

■ Don't forget gasoline credit cards. These can pay for more than fuel. Your wife can charge tires, car repairs, and other fees to your account.

■ If you're renting, stop paying the rent. Let her worry about it, as you'll be moving out to another residence. If you skip a couple of rent payments, you can begin building up a cash reserve, which you may need to pay your additional expenses.

■ If paying off a mortgage on a house, stop making payments. She'll be the one facing eviction.

■ Take the family car with you, especially if it's in your name, to leave her without transportation.

■ Cancel your life insurance, so that if anything happens to you, she won't profit by your death. You'll need whatever equity you've built into the plan.

■ If there are two cars in your name alone, sell one if you have the time. The other choice is to cancel the insurance on it, if you live in a state with mandatory auto insurance. Be very careful before you do this, because it can be a booby-trap for you. Consult your lawyer, first. If state law requires the insurance company to notify the motor vehicle bureau of any change in coverage, and the bureau revokes the registration if insurance is dropped, you can take away her transportation. If it's illegal to drive an uninsured vehicle, it's a double whammy for her. However, the problem comes because the car is in your name. If she gets into an accident, you may still be liable, and that can kick back at you. This is why you must, repeat, must, consult your lawyer before you make this sort of move.

One way to help the situation along, in a mandatory insurance state, is to remove the license plates. This will get her stopped by the first cop who notices. When he checks her registration and motor vehicle insurance, she'll be effectively "grounded." She may even have to pay a fine.

Do not make the error of reporting the car stolen. You'll have to identify yourself when making the report, and you'll find that both police and the penal code frown on providing false information to police.

■ Cancel her health insurance if she's carried on your policy. This is most effective if she needs regular medical care, and if you're a member of a health maintenance organization, where they'll stop accepting her card after you cancel. She'll have to get her own insurance, and this can be extremely difficult, especially if she has a "pre-existing condition." The current health insurance crisis makes it worse.

This is an extremely nasty trick, and can be very effective as a harassment tactic, because some doctors won't accept patients without health insurance, or the ability to pay "up front." Paying in cash will deplete her cash reserve.

■ Retain the house keys. Make her pay a locksmith to change the locks if she wants to be spiteful and lock you out.

■ Cancel utilities to your address, effective on the day you move. Ideally, you should move on a Friday, so that your wife will be stranded during the weekend without electricity, telephone, water, etc.

■ Cancel all other services to your address, mainly so that you won't be billed for them. This includes newspaper delivery, cable service, etc. If she wants them, she'll have to have them reinstated at her expense.

■ As soon as you see the break-up coming, defer all repairs possible on household equipment, and don't buy any replacement items. For example, if the washer or air conditioner appear to be on their last legs, don't repair or replace them. Save your money and leave her with the costs of repair or replacement.

■ If you jointly own a house, and the property tax bill comes to you, don't pay it. Let her worry about being dispossessed. Of course, you're both legally liable for it, due to joint ownership, but if you don't pay, the worst that can happen to you personally is a cash penalty. If the county takes over the house for unpaid taxes, she can get evicted.

■ Reduce your liability insurance, if you jointly own a house and she is now living in it rent-free. You probably were paying for enough liability insurance to protect your total assets, but now you don't care if you lose the house in a lawsuit.

■ A good reason for not procrastinating is that the Social Security Administration considers a 10-year marriage as qualifying for payments, in case of divorce, and will pay benefits to a divorced wife at age 65 if the ex-husband dies first. She can collect at any age, if caring for an "entitled" child (under 16 or disabled) of the deceased worker. If you're close to the ten-year mark, have no under-16 children by your present wife, and you are contemplating a divorce, make sure it goes through before you hit that magic number. This simple step will cut her off from benefits forever.

Sources

1. *Women and Money*, Mary Rogers and Nancy Joyce, New York, McGraw-Hill, 1978, p. 156.

2. *Child Support*, Marianne Takas, New York, Harper & Row, 1985, p. 70.

3. *Women and Money*, pp. 162-163.

10

Custody And
Child Support

As we've seen, the rate of divorce has increased over the long haul in the United States. The number of children involved has also increased. There were 299,000 children involved in divorces in 1950, and by 1960 the number had risen to 463,000. In 1970, 870,000 children were involved, and in 1972 the number topped a million for the first time, with the exact total at 1,021,000. In 1975, there were 1,123,000 children involved, and by 1986 the number had dropped slightly, to 1,064,000.

The unfortunate and tragic fact about children whose parents separate is that they're liable to be pawns, bargaining counters, and hostages in the process. Married partners tend to use children against each other. At best, there's bound to be a conflict of loyalties for the child or children.

Courts state piously that they make custody decisions "in the best interests of the child." Realistically, they follow both law and tradition.

We know that wives usually obtain custody of the children. Some women look forward to this, because it's a fail-safe way of extorting support payments from their ex-husbands. Unfortunately, not all biological mothers are fit mothers. A peculiarity of our society is that people, including judges, will often accept the mother's allegations regarding the father's unfitness at face value, but demand proof of any charges against the mother.

An important reason for this is that judges are elected, or subject to recall. They don't want to make decisions that will get women's groups against them at election time.

In one case brought to the author's attention by the father, the mother had played sexual games with both pre-teen boys, and a teen-age girl placed with the family by the county foster parents program. County officials later withdrew the girl when it became apparent that the mother was abusing her, but were unable to get enough evidence to make a criminal charge stick. The father had tried to prosecute for sexual conduct with the two boys, to have her declared unfit, but the wife's lawyer was very skilled and very aggressive, and managed to thwart that. A point worth noting, however, was that this took place over twenty years ago, when a child's testimony didn't count for much, and before the current wave of "child abuse" hysteria had begun.

In another, and more recent case, the main issue in the divorce was custody of the couple's two children, a seven-year-old boy and a three-year-old-girl. The husband wanted sole custody, because he felt that his wife was unfit, because of her drinking and night-clubbing. The wife opposed this, and accused her husband of sexually molesting their boy. She told her attorney that the boy had told her that the husband has "played with him" one day when they were alone. The husband's response was to request polygraph examinations for both himself and his wife. The judge ordered them both to undergo such testing, but the day before the scheduled tests, the wife confessed her fabrication.

The husband had spent thousands of dollars on psychiatrists and psychologists, to produce testimony that his wife was unfit and that the children would be harmed. These "experts" testified for two days, and the wife's attorney offered no rebuttal at the end. The judge's decision went against the husband, nevertheless, and the wife got the children. The reason? As the husband later discovered, the wife's attorney was the judge's father-in-law.

Sometimes, it boils down to who can take better care of the children. Even though judges normally assume that the mother is the natural parent for custody, some factors can upset this calculation, if you know how to play your cards correctly. Unless you're very affluent, you simply won't earn enough to support two households, and your ex-wife will have to work. This means that she'll be a part-time parent, overcoming one of the objections against granting you custody. If you move in with your mother, sister, or even have a live-in female companion, you'll have the best of both worlds. You'll have a family member to take care of the children while you're away at work, while the best your ex-wife might manage would be a day care center.

Joint Custody

Abuses by divorced mothers have become so flagrant, and so common, that they're forcing changes in the way the law treats the question of custody. A new development in the child custody field is the concept of joint custody, in which parents take equal responsibility for the care of the children, and share their time equally or jointly. At least thirty states have adopted joint custody laws.

California's joint custody law, adopted in 1980, states that "there shall be a presumption... that joint custody is in the best interest of the child." It also allows joint custody if only one parent requests it. At least seven states have followed this lead.

This is a definite step forward in correcting the imbalance in divorce laws.

Using Children Against the Father

In states with divorce for cause, wives can use the children directly against their husbands. It's easy for a wife to coach her young children to make negative statements against their father. Remember that, typically, the mother remains at home with the children while the father is out working. This fosters a closer relationship, because the father is a relative stranger, and the mother finds it easier than the father to manipulate the children. If the issue is emotional brutality, or some such, children may be part of the wife's case against the husband.

Another problem comes with the mother poisoning children's minds against the father. Young children are impressionable, and some mothers teach them to hate the father.

False Accusations

The nastiest thing that can happen with children is to find your spouse accusing you of child abuse or molestation. This is such an emotionally charged subject that an accusation equals guilt. Of course, a child abuse charge brings a prison term only if a court finds you guilty. However, the effect such a charge can have upon you among your friends, and on the job, is devastating.

There have been instances of husbands falsely accused of child abuse by spouses, simply as a way of striking back at them.[1] A charge will hold up long enough to cause you a lot of grief, because you'll have to hire a criminal lawyer to defend you. You'll find yourself besieged on several fronts, because the outcome of the divorce or child custody hearing will depend upon the outcome of the criminal investigation. This, in turn, will depend upon the outcome of an investigation by the state "child protection agency," which may or may not be fair in the way it treats you.

If all goes well, and the court grants you visitation rights, your troubles may not be over yet. A powerful weapon that an ex-wife can use to deny her ex-husband visitation is a manufactured charge of child abuse or molestation. This is something she can initiate at any time after the court grants you visitation, because the time frame doesn't matter. If she gets mad at you a month, or a year later, she can bring an accusation. She may tell the court that her daughter has begun to "act strangely" after a visit with you. If she tells the child welfare officer that she will be taking the child to a psychologist, this can result in your being denied visitation until the psychologist provides a report. This can take months, or even a year.

Some young children provide damaging testimony against an accused adult as a result of coaching by parents and over-zealous investigators. Some investigators are so convinced that an accused adult is automatically guilty that they'll ask leading questions, and even badger the child until he or she says what they want to hear. The case may eventually fail in court, but meanwhile the defendant will have gone through hell.

The reason is that the criminal justice system hits hardest at law-abiding, middle-class persons. A hardened felon can waltz around the "system," because he knows the weaknesses and loopholes built into it. He knows that the system will provide him with an attorney if he can't afford to hire one. The law-abiding citizen with a steady job and some savings will find his finances devastated by the need to defend himself against a criminal charge. The prosecutor can spend a lot of time building a case, and allocate many resources, while the defendant's resources are limited. If the defendant is not indigent, he'll see his life savings eroded by the need to pay a defense lawyer, who bills by the hour. This is true whether the defendant is guilty or innocent.

If you're unfortunate enough to have this happen to you, keep in mind that it may not be as bad as it first appears. Although an accusation of child abuse is highly emotional, and can alienate you at work and in the community, some people will take it with a grain of salt. The police, for example, will wonder about a charge that crops up just when you're filing for divorce, or after the court has awarded you visitation. Likewise, both your attorney and the judge will probably have heard such charges before. Police investigators will be asking your wife some pointed questions, relating to when she first became aware of the alleged abuse, and why she didn't report it until now. Under close questioning, a concocted story can fall apart. If the "system" works well, the consequences can rebound against your ex-wife. Judges don't like people who mess with them.

Whatever the case, never plead guilty. Your lawyer may try to push you into a plea agreement, where you plead guilty in return for a reduced charge or sentence, but never do this if you're innocent, as it will make you look guilty. If your lawyer insists you cop a plea, get another lawyer.

If Your Wife Is Pregnant

You ought to be aware of the effects of alcohol, nicotine, and illegal drugs upon unborn children. If your wife uses any of these, and she's pregnant, when the divorce action is pending, you should consider steps to protect the baby.

Also consider the double-barrel effect of this as a legal harassment tactic. During one divorce action in Tennessee, the husband requested that his wife be forced to submit to periodic drug/alcohol testing until the birth of the baby. In another case, a judge ordered the wife jailed to keep her away from drug use until the baby was born. This tactic has teeth in it, as women have been successfully prosecuted in this country for endangering their unborn children by using drugs. This has happened in Miami, Florida, Greenville, South Carolina, and elsewhere.

Visitation Rights

Some ex-wives are very possessive about their children, and will deny visitation by the father. Others do it out of spite, just as many wives automatically change the locks after the husband leaves home. Even though the father has certain "rights," under the court decree, enforcing these is another matter, because courts typically give the benefit of every doubt to the mother. This is the result of a barrage of propaganda from the feminist side. Many of the recent feminist books dealing with divorce and the divorced mother take a very derogatory tone towards husbands, as well as men in general. These have influenced legislators and judges.

In one sense, you have leverage in that you can withhold child support payments, but in reality this is an empty gun. Courts are typically stricter in enforcing the mothers' and children's rights than the fathers' rights, and you can get in trouble even by threatening to withhold payments. Also, withholding payments can deprive your children, and you can be sure that your ex-wife will play this up for all the "guilt" it's worth. In court, she and her lawyer will make you look like an inhuman monster.

In some cases, a written agreement serves to define each parent's rights regarding visitations, and other custody matters. However, this can also serve as a harassment tool by your ex-wife, because the agreement can be so detailed, and lay so many obligations on you, that you can't abide by it. One possibility, for the sake of "safety," is to require children to use seat belts.[2] Although this appears reasonable on the surface, other stipulations may not be. Enough of these conditions can make you look like an irresponsible parent, and a violator, because it'll be impossible to meet them all. If this is coupled with an agreement that attorney fees for any future actions to enforce the agreement will be paid by the parent violating the agreement, this lays a trap for you because it's a no-win situation.

There are other booby-traps women try to insert into any child-custody agreement. One is that, although you're the one making the payments, she gets the children as deductions on her tax return.[3] Federal law already mandates that the custodial parent has the deduction, but this is just another way of sticking it to the father twice over.

Enforcing Child Support

The Federal Child Support Enforcement Program is the result of a law passed by Congress in 1975. This is a complex program to enforce child support decrees, taking in state and local government agencies in what's supposed to be a coordinated effort to extract child support payments from delinquent fathers.[4]

This is an example of a law passed for one purpose being twisted to serve another. This legislation was originally designed to deal with "lower income families."[5] This phrase is "governmentalese," and a euphemism for minority people who bore children out of wedlock. Typically, the father would impregnate the mother and move on to another woman when he became aware of the pregnancy. The mother would go on welfare, and the purpose of the federal program was to reduce the costs of federal "Aid to Families with Dependent Children," or AFDC. The new law created the Office of Child Support Enforcement,

OCSE, to track down fathers and make them pay for the support of their biological children.

Unfortunately, you can't get blood from a stone. Many of the people originally targeted by this law were in the lowest economic groups, with the highest unemployment rates. It's hard to extract support payments from an unemployed father. The net result has been that only fathers with means have been vulnerable to this type of enforcement. Techniques used to collect child support have included requiring fathers to post cash bonds, reporting violators to credit agencies, seizing their property, garnishing their paychecks, and confiscating their tax refund checks.[6] Obviously, these methods are meaningless against indigents. They're also very difficult to enforce against a man who denies paternity.[7]

Grasping and greedy ex-wives, however, saw this as an easy way to extort support payments from ex-husbands, because the program is available at nominal charge to mothers not on welfare. Previously, a mother would have had to hire a lawyer to start proceedings for collection. Now, there are even several books in print explaining step-by-step procedures for nailing the father, establishing paternity, and squeezing money from him.[8]

The threat of jail, as we'll see, is real but remote. A loudmouth wife or ex-wife may threaten the husband with jail, but this has severe drawbacks. One, about which women care little, is that the father is deprived of due-process.[9]

Another technique, however, gives the wife a green light to loot her husband's resources. A complaint to the Internal Revenue Service can result in withholding her husband's refund check, and the wife can have the money turned over to her. The husband is entitled to a hearing, but only weeks after the wife has received the money. In one case, the wife had falsely accused her ex-husband of defaulting on child support payments, and received $1,200 due him in a tax refund. At the hearing, the husband produced receipts and canceled checks to prove that he had not failed to make the payments, but the IRS officials told him that he'd have to recover the money from his wife, because the IRS had already handed over the money to her. This appeared problematic, as his wife had already spent it. This left him with no recourse. The IRS was unwilling to prosecute the ex-wife for making false statements, and the court informed him that he could deduct the amount from the tail end of the support payments, just before the children reached maturity. IRS officials also informed the husband that his wife could do the same thing to him again the following year, and that there was nothing they could do about it.

Custodial Abuses by the Mother

Let's quickly look at some tactics that separated and divorced mothers use against the father. Some of these are illegal, but proving them is another problem. Most are borderline, and proving the abuse is practically impossible.

Impeding Visitation

Denying ordered visitation is illegal. However, there are ways for the mother to make it very hard on you. One is simply not having the children ready on time, and making you wait outside for an hour while she "prepares" or "dresses" them.

In some cases, a determined ex-wife can sabotage visitation arrangements, secure in the knowledge that the law hits harder at husbands who withhold support payments. In one case, the mother sent both children out of state before her ex-husband arrived for his scheduled visitation. When he complained to her, she told him boldly; "Go to the court." He did complain to the court, but it took three months to schedule a hearing, by which time the issue was moot. The judge simply told the wife sternly not to repeat the behavior, but imposed no sanctions. She knew that she would be able to get away with it next time, as well.

Impeding Communication With Children

Your wife may intercept and destroy letters you send to your children, or refuse to let you speak with them on the phone. She may also cut short any telephone calls you make to them, leaving you holding a dead phone.

Incurring Unnecessary Expenses

We all know that, even for essential goods and services, there are ways to economize, as well as ways to run up bills. Shopping at an expensive supermarket, and saving the receipts to document a need for more money, is an example of the latter. Another is jacking up medical bills. Many medical services are optional or elective, but choosing them for the children will cause extra expenses. A vengeful wife can take the children to the doctor for "checkups" at a time she knows her ex-husband is strapped. It's also possible to run up fantastic bills with an orthodontist, at your expense.

Legal Harassment

Your ex-wife may choose to take all issues to court, instead of trying to settle them informally with you first. If you're ordered to pay both attorney's fees, it's no-risk for her, and no-win for you.

Economic Self-Defense

You may be making the payments you can afford, and these may be just enough to support the children. On the other hand, if you're affluent, you may feel that your wife and her lawyer have jacked up the payments to far more than what she really needs, so that she may live the high life at your expense. Unfortunately, proving this is difficult, and always time-consuming.

You may also find yourself victimized if you provide support without adequately documenting it. One child support advocate advises divorced mothers to keep a meticulous record of child support payment amounts and dates, as a way of documenting any failure to pay.[10] This is why you need to protect yourself. A woman can easily "forget" to record a cash payment, or the value of a gift, or even the fact that you took care of some bills for her when she was having a hard time.

One obvious point is never to hand over cash without obtaining a receipt on the spot. Better yet, always pay by check, which produces proof that your ex-wife indeed collected the amount.

A greedy ex-wife may also try to squeeze more out of you than the court has allowed, by wheedling "extras" and taking advantage of your trying to be a nice guy. She may also ask for a few dollars in cash, to pay a doctor's bill, or to buy a pair of shoes for one of the children. You may hand over some cash, and not even keep a record of how much it adds up to over a year or two. After you've bought the children extra toys, or taken them and your ex-wife to dinner a few times, you may get the feeling that this should be deducted from your support payments or alimony. That's how they play GOTCHA.

A request for the children's benefit is practically irresistible, and you will usually want to give her the benefit of the doubt. However, always remember to collect a receipt for anything you give, and if requests become excessive, inform your ex-wife that you're going to use these receipts to substantiate a request for reduction of payments. Better yet, ask the court before you lay out one red cent.

We've already examined ways of ducking payments if you're willing to go for broke, and disappear. These are drastic methods, and require drastic changes in your life. There's also a range of softer methods available. These don't have as immediate an effect, and require almost as much attention to detail. You'll have to use one or more of these methods of economic survival if you wish to remain in the area, or keep in contact with relatives and friends.

Probably the best way, if you live in a state allowing joint custody, is to threaten your wife with it. This is a good bargaining position when allowed by law. You force your wife and her attorney to make the painful choice of accepting reduced payments or having to face a joint custody fight with you.[11] This is excellent strategy, because, frankly, it's also emotional blackmail. This makes it a legitimate weapon to use in a situation in which women often blackmail men.

Naturally, you're still subject to the woman's blackmail, that any action you take to reduce your payments will take food right out of the mouths of your kids. There is a way to handle this without taking food out of their mouths. You push for a concession allowing you to pay it all as alimony. This allows you to deduct it on your tax return, while your wife can claim the children as exemptions. It's fair. It helps both parties. For these two reasons, you'll probably have trouble getting your wife to accept it. The reason is the wife's hidden agenda of making it hard on you. Support payments are punitive, and are designed to cripple your finances, remember? Your wife won't be eager to give you a break, even though it doesn't cost her a cent.

Joint custody, if the court awards it, is also useful as economic blackmail. You maintain that, because you'll be supporting the child or children for part of the year, your ex-wife won't need as much money for their support. This is an excellent lever for reducing support payments. The logic is impeccable, and should pass through any court, unless the judge is a feminist.

Impeding collection is another tactic. One way to make it difficult for your ex-wife to collect is to move to another state. This can be just across the state line. However, there is a provision for interstate collection of child support payments; the Uniform Reciprocal Enforcement of Support Act or URESA. This system has two weaknesses. One is that the ex-wife must furnish the father's current address, which she may not know. The other is that, like any bureaucracy, the system takes time to act. What works in your favor is that a moving target is hard to hit.

You can also remain in the area and get payments reduced. Although your ex-wife has most of the cards, you still have a few aces up your sleeve. The basic fact is that your ex-wife and the court need your active cooperation to obtain these payments. The corollary is that your ex-wife needs the money more than she needs you in jail. This is the key, and the court will go along with you if you make your moves deftly. Your ex-wife may protest vehemently, but the judge knows that, if he sends you to jail, the money flow stops.

There are several legal ways to have child support payments reduced or suspended by the court. One is to reduce your income. You can't simply quit your job, because the judge can throw you in jail for contempt of court. Illness will serve as an excuse. It doesn't have to be physical illness, as you can state that the divorce, and separation from your children, have left you depressed. Presenting this to the court as grounds for reducing payments almost always works.

Likewise if you go for counseling, and are not covered by a health plan. You can present the court with a choice of allowing you to divert money for counseling to help you continue to work, or risk having you unable to work because it denied you the care you needed.

If you're self-employed, you have more control over what you earn. You can easily manipulate your affairs so that, at least, your income doesn't rise, and then you can gradually reduce it. The economy is always fluctuating, and some of the reasons you can cite for your income decline are:

- Business slow-down.

Your industry is going through a down-turn, and business is slow right now. The down-turn may be seasonal, such as a winter slump in air-conditioner sales. After the slow-down, business does not pick-up, for various reasons.

- Recession.

This is easier to document, as national economic index figures are public information. The recession offers you a quick and easy answer if the judge asks when you'll be able to resume the previous high level of support payments: "When the recession ends."

- Depression.

Same as recession, but more severe.

Whatever you do, you must also reduce your assets. The reason is that the court may seize your car, house, furniture, etc., if you fall behind in payments. This is partly to ensure that your ex-wife receives the money awarded by the court, and partly to punish you for the delinquency. Make no mistake about it: punishment is part of the system. Therefore, if you have little or nothing to seize, the court will be frustrated.

One interesting variation is if you live in a part of the country where an automobile is essential for transportation. If the court seizes your car, you can't get to work. If you need your car for your work, such as outside sales, taking your car means destroying your earning power. Make sure you drive an inexpensive car. If you drive a BMW or Mercedes, the judge may order you to sell it and buy a Chevy.

Punitiveness can backfire. One hard-nosed judge set support payments exceeding the husband's income. When the husband pointed this out to him, the judge advised him to get a part-time job. The husband left the state, and today his ex-wife is getting nothing.

With all of these moves, you place your ex-wife, her attorney, and the judge on the horns of a dilemma. While appearing to be cooperative, you become less able to pay. It's easy for your ex-wife's attorney and the judge to understand that, although partial payments are unsatisfactory, they're better than getting nothing at all, which would be the case if you were in jail.

Sources

1. *A Question of Innocence*, Lawrence D. Spiegel, NJ, Unicorn Publishing House, 1986. This book is the story of a psychologist who was accused of molesting his two-year-old daughter. The accusation came from his ex-wife. The state child protection agency and the police were her unwitting accomplices in bringing the husband to court on criminal charges. During the trials, it became evident how the case had been fabricated, the child coached to give false testimony, and several professional investigators fooled in the process.

   Also see: *Divorced Father*, Gerald A. Hill, Ph. D., White Hall, VA, Better Way Publications, 1989, pp. 55-70. The book's author was himself the subject of a false charge of child molestation, and he describes in great detail how it's possible to take advantage of credulous and naive child-welfare workers and manufacture an accusation out of nothing. He also describes the steps involved in countering such a charge, pointing out that, if it gets to the stage of criminal charges, the accused should never accept any sort of "deal" or plea agreement, because that equals an acceptance of guilt.

Another book dealing with child sexual abuse points out that there's been a rash of false accusations in conjunction with divorce actions. See *Nap Time*, by Lisa Manshell, New York, William Morrow and Company, 1990, p. 23.

2. *Child Support*, Marianne Takas, Harper & Row, 1985, p. 125.

3. *Ibid.*, p. 134.

4. *Child Support Survivor's Guide*, Barry T. Schnell, Salem, NJ, Consumer Awareness Learning Laboratory, 1984, p. 18.

5. *Child Support*, p. xii.

6. *Ibid.*, p. 8.

7. *Child Support Survivor's Guide*, pp. 27-28.

8. One such book, written by a women's advocate, is: *Child Support*, Marianne Takas, Harper & Row, 1985. This explains in great detail how to use government agencies to obtain money from the father, how to use criminal enforcement, how to ferret out the father's entire financial picture, and how to use this information for best effect. A resources section in the back of this book lists a variety of women's organizations, but none concerned with father's rights.

Another book, this one written by a man, is: *Child Support Survivor's Guide*, Barry T. Schnell, cited above. This one is also slanted against husbands. An example is a listing of "excuses" fathers give for not paying. Another is a section titled "The Man — A Child Support Victim," in which the author lists reasons why many men feel that they don't get a fair shake from the courts, and then dismisses them.

9. *Making Fathers Pay: The Enforcement of Child Support*, David Chambers, Chicago, IL, University of Chicago Press, 1979.

10. *Child Support*, pp. 168-170.

11. *The Equality Trap*, Mary Ann Mason, Simon and Schuster, 1988, p. 83.

11

Your Home Away From Home

The odds are that you will be the one to move out, not your wife. This is especially true if there are children.

Moving out can be easy, if you have nothing but a few clothes, a shaving kit, and your wallet. Some husbands can move out with little effort, and live out of their cars for awhile, although this certainly isn't the most comfortable thing to do. On the other hand, if you've accumulated half a lifetime's belongings, you'll find moving out a chore, and perhaps even a backbreaking task.

Planning is the key to a successful move, whether open or clandestine. You may feel that a clandestine move is better, for several reasons, but you need to plan either way.

If the move will be open, you may need to reach agreement with your spouse regarding what you will take. It can be awkward to hire movers and have their work held up because of a disagreement at the time of the move. You can, however, call the cops if she tries to prevent you from moving when the big truck arrives.

You may decide to do it without telling her in advance, or even telling her at all, letting it come as a surprise.

Why not? This can be justifiable if your wife has an explosive temper, or if she is irrational. An excellent reason for doing this is if you fear she may harm the children, or destroy your property. Yet another good reason is if she's a chronic liar. If you tell her first, she might go to court to swear out an injunction against you, as we've already seen. In such a case, the ideal move is one made while she's away and after which she returns to find you and your things gone.

Yet another reason is purely defensive: you don't want to tip your hand. This means moving as much as you can without her noticing. If you have a lot of books, for example, you should be able to transfer some of them without leaving conspicuous gaps on the bookshelves. If you've been able to afford renting an apartment, you can move your stuff directly. If paying rent for several weeks or months is too much for you, rent a storage room, as a convenient drop-off point until you find new quarters.

Remember also that packing and moving some items yourself will save both time and money on moving day. It's possible to hire a moving crew to come in and pack five hundred dishes, crystal goblets, and various works of art, so that they won't be damaged during transport. It's also damned expensive. Unless you have a lot of money to spend, you'll find that moving small and portable items yourself saves you a lot.

The first step is to make a list of everything you want to take with you. This includes personal effects, such as clothing, business records, and furniture. You'll also find other items worth including, if you can take them, because replacing them may be expensive. This is the crucial point. Original price isn't as important as replacement value, especially if an item is something you need in daily life.

You need to keep this in mind for the following reason: It may happen that the first thing your wife will do after finding you gone is to change the locks, not so much because she's afraid of you, but to keep you from returning for anything you may have forgotten. This is pure spite, but it's happened to many men.

Make a separate personal effects list for each person you're taking with you. Remember that, if you move the kids out, you'll also have to move their clothing, toys, and other items.

You may save time and trouble if you don't need some of the items on your list. Moving to a furnished apartment will relieve you of the need to include furniture, except perhaps bedding. If you always eat out, you may not need any kitchen items, unless you acquire a live-in girlfriend who likes to cook for you.

However, remember that every item you take with you will save you money at the other end. Bedsheets and bath mats aren't very valuable in themselves, and their cash value is very small, especially second-hand. If, however, you have to buy these items to set yourself up in your new pad, you'll have to lay out replacement value, not depreciated value.

A point to remember is to do your laundry and dry cleaning before your move. You may not have a washer and dryer conveniently at hand where you're going. Also keep in mind that an apartment complex with coin-operated laundry facilities can be very convenient for residents.

Apartment Hunting

Once you've decided what you want to keep, you can begin looking for new quarters. Some men move in with parents or other relatives. Others may room with a fellow employee, or a friend seeking to share an apartment or house. This makes the logistics easier, but you may not be as lucky, and may have to find an apartment.

Apartment hunting can be difficult, depending on the area. One reason is that real estate agents and apartment managers in many instances appear to be "losers" who are unable to hold other employment because they're generally inept. You may encounter some who are late for appointments, or don't know whom to call to have utilities turned on. Others are drunk or mysteriously absent during posted office hours. Some don't even have business cards! Part of your search will be spent simply looking for a rental agent who is "all there" upstairs.

The more time you have to look, the better off you'll be. Trying to get relocated in a hurry is a lot of hassle, and if you have to move out within a few days, your work-load will be crushing.

A few factors can narrow your choices.

Rent

How much can you afford? Keep in mind that you'll need "front money" to move, including a security deposit, the first month's rent, and moving expenses. You'll also need to spend money on incidentals, such as stocking the refrigerator. If you can afford to eat out every day, you're probably affluent enough not to have to worry much about expenses.

Location

How far from your work-place do you want to be? If you work in or near the city center, you may find that rents close-in are higher than those farther away, and that you'll have to trade off rent against commuting time. Also think about how far you'll be from your former home. If you hate your wife and never want to see her again, you don't care. If you have children, and want to see them regularly, you'll want to be close enough to avoid a long trip. If you're taking the kids with you, you'll need to locate a day-care center for their care while you're away at work.

Space

Will you be alone, or do you also need to take someone with you? Perhaps you'll also be moving a 90-year-old mother who's been living with you. Maybe you want a spare bedroom so that you can have the kids with you overnight. If you're taking the kids with you, you'll definitely need another bedroom, because the judge will be scrutinizing their living accommodations very closely when deciding who gets custody. Perhaps you need an extra room an as office or work-room if you have a hobby or operate a business at home. You may want a two-car garage, both for your car and as a work-room. You must consider the need for extra space before choosing an apartment or house.

Transferring Utilities and Services

Another step you'll have to take in advance is transferring your telephone and electric service. As we've pointed out in a previous chapter, it's far easier if all services are in your name, not your wife's. Let's see why.

If your wife has been excruciatingly nasty, you can leave her in blissful ignorance until the day after you've left, when the electricity goes off and the phone stops working. She'll have to scramble to get service restored, using a neighbor's phone and trying to establish credit with the utilities. Be careful, however, because a nasty wife can make this appear to be a vindictive action on your part. Ask your attorney about this before you make your move.

You'll also save yourself time and hassle if you simply have to transfer services rather than if you're a new subscriber. If you've been paying the electric bill in your own name at the same address for the last ten years, the electric company isn't going to ask you for references or run a credit check on you. Likewise, the telephone company will have you listed as an established customer.

New subscribers often have to front a deposit before the electric or telephone company will begin service. You're going to have enough expenses making your move, and don't need this. One fee which you may have to pay is for transfer of service. This may easily be fifty dollars.

When a utility company transfers service, it stops providing the service at the old address. This is standard procedure, and a crucial point for you, because you don't want to be responsible for services she'll use. She may easily make hundreds of dollars of long-distance calls on your account, after you've left.

Obviously, you can't transfer services until you have your new address. You'll also have to give your local Post Office a change-of-address card. The change-of-address card is an important step if you're not sure that your wife will hold your mail for you to pick up. Your wife, if she's spiteful, may simply destroy some envelopes whose loss she thinks will hurt you most. With the postal service the way it is today, there's no way you can prove they were ever delivered. You have to take care of these details before the actual move, because there's always a delay in transferring services.

If your telephone calls are important to you, it's vital to transfer the telephone service, instead of leaving it in your former residence. The reason is that if you leave the phone the way it is, and apply for a new number, you'll have to notify all of your friends and business contacts of your new number. If you take the phone service with you, you'll continue to receive your calls. Even if your new residence is too far away for you to retain the same number, the telephone company will put a taped message on your old line, to advise callers of your new number. This service lasts only a couple of months, though. Another reason, if your wife is vindictive, is to prevent her playing games with your telephone calls.

This point can be extremely important. If you receive many business calls, your wife may tell callers that you're dead, in prison, out of state, etc., and sabotage relations with your clients and contacts.

One final point to check, in regard to your telephone service, is whether the telephone company will provide you with directories at your new address. This is usually automatic, but sometimes you have to request them.

If the separation has been amicable, you can arrange to have utilities continued at your present address for a few days after you've left, to give her time to have them started in her own name. You can also inform her of the cut-off date, to make it easier on her.

Another matter is your house or apartment keys. There's no reason to hand them over to her, unless you want to be nice. You're not even likely to be forced to do so by a court order, because any judge will know that you may easily have had them duplicated. Retaining your keys forces her to have the locks changed, at a time when her spare cash will be low.

Choosing a Mover

You have to be careful in choosing a mover, as they're not equal. Some are simply careless, because they know that people don't move very often, and they don't care about repeat business. Others, however, are conscientious. A good mover can make your task a lot easier during a difficult moment.

The best way of finding a good mover is to ask friends, acquaintances, and fellow employees who have recently moved, for recommendations. Let their experiences guide you, and don't base your decision on price alone.

Generally, the mover will charge you an hourly fee, for a truck and crew. For local moves, the crew may be only two or three men. The mover will provide boxes, and cardboard wardrobes for clothing, charging for each one. The moving crew will even do the packing for you, if you wish. This will result in an extra charge. This is why the more you can pack and move yourself, the less expensive it will be.

Try to get an estimate from the mover's sales rep. For this, you need a detailed list of exactly what you need moved. If you can't do this, simply ask for their hourly rate, and calculate a half-hour for each room you need moved, add the travel time, and total the figures. This isn't the best way, but at least it will provide a rough comparison between movers.

A Moving Checklist

- Set-up your own separate bank account.
- Find a new house or apartment.
- Rent extra storage space if you will need it.
- Find a suitable day care center, if applicable.
- Arrange for change of:
  - ☐ Telephone
  - ☐ Mailing address
  - ☐ Electricity
  - ☐ Cable TV service
  - ☐ Drivers License Bureau notification
  - ☐ Car registration.
- Get forms to cancel services to your old residence, or have them put in your wife's name.
- Move small items in advance.
- Arrange for moving services or truck rental.
- Pack as much as possible before the big day arrives.
- Get your laundry done.

After The Move

If you've left on good terms, you may be able to return to pick up anything you inadvertently left behind during the move. Otherwise, you'll have to face the possibility that your wife will have locked you out, or trashed anything that's yours.

You may have to replace a few items, such as furniture, which you didn't take with you but now feel you need. Second-hand furniture will do for a start, especially if your future plans are uncertain. You may decide to leave the state, or the country, in which case it's pointless to tie up money in expensive furniture.

Also keep in mind that you may have to do a lot of hurried food buying. You might choose to eat out, but that's even more expensive. To help you shop, it's easiest to make a list of all the foods in your house before you move out: everything in the refrigerator, cupboards, pantry, etc. Don't just list "spices" or "cereal." Spell out exact items and brand names — it will make your shopping a lot easier.

You'll probably be buying your immediate needs at the closest supermarket, without much attention to price. This is acceptable if you've got plenty of money, but if cash is tight, you'll have to make the most of every dollar.

As a man, you may not have had much recent experience in shopping supermarkets, and will be vulnerable to some of their economic sucker-punches. If you try to shop sale items, you may get fooled by a very common trick; putting signs on items that are not actually on sale. These signs have headings such as; "Discount Priced," "Compare Our Price," and "Price Saver." Supermarket managers take advantage of the fact that many people don't read signs carefully, or simply assume that if there's a sign on an item, it must be on sale. Also be wary of coupons that appear in newspapers. These are time-wasters because they offer a few cents off on a jacked-up price. If you can't resist the temptation to clip coupons, always compare what you're considering buying with competitive items, to see if the cents-off coupon actually affords you a lower price than buying something else at the regular price.

Another point to watch, after leaving home, is not to do anything that your wife can use against you. This is especially true if she's nasty, vindictive, or paranoid. You may telephone her to request something, but if she gets nasty and hangs up, don't call her back, however angry you might be. Judges tend to believe wives' claims that their husbands are making "harassing" phone calls.

12

The Price
of Liberty

Can you afford to get divorced? For the very rich, and the very poor, the answer is almost always "yes." The reason is obvious for the very rich. They can afford extremely costly legal fights, millions in settlements and alimony payments, and still maintain their opulent lifestyles. The very poor have two choices: formal divorce, or simply leaving. A divorce for the very poor can come about with the help of the paper "divorce kits" that are legal in some states, or through the help of the Legal Aid Society. Divorce for anyone at the very bottom of the economic scale is bound to be quick, because there's no property to cause long negotiations, and no money to pay lawyers for drawn-out litigation.

Walking out on a bad marriage is the choice of many of the down-and-out. It's practical because an angry and vengeful spouse cannot effectively pursue them. This is true even if there are child support payments in the picture, because for all practical purposes, it's out of the question to try to squeeze them out of a randomly employed unskilled worker. A judge may issue an order, but the husband has to be within reach and earning a paycheck to make it effective. Jail merely confines the husband; it doesn't produce support payments or put food on the table.

Recently, in Phoenix, Arizona, a judge adopted a "get tough" policy against child-support deadbeats. He collected well over a dozen men whom he considered hard-core non-payers, and threatened them with jail if they did not cough up the money. One was a dentist, and the others were also affluent. Another vulnerability was that they were well-established in the community, and had a lot to lose if the judge put them in jail for days or weeks. The program was so well-publicized that he promised to repeat it for Valentine's Day. He did, and obtained even greater publicity, which suggests that the judge might have political ambitions. However, this approach won't work with the person who has little or nothing, and drifts from job to job.

You can't suck blood from a stone. A man who drifts from town to town, working as a laborer or dishwasher for a couple of weeks before moving on, is an elusive target. By the time a judge can get a warrant into the hands of the local sheriff, the target has relocated.

Those in the middle class are the ones who suffer most, because they cannot get free legal counsel, and have enough property to make it worthwhile for a wife to conduct protracted litigation to obtain a piece of it. When a family breaks apart, the same total income now has to pay for two domiciles. There's also the cost of time lost from work, the costs of moving, attorney's fees, and many other incidentals that add up to a respectable total. A general rule is that, after a divorce, both parties suffer a decline in standard of living.

Let's start calculating how much a divorce may cost you.

Attorney's Fees

There are two variables: his hourly rate and how complicated the case is. As in other fields, you cannot judge an attorney's skill by the fees he charges. Some beginners, charging low fees, will try very hard for you, because they want to make names for themselves. A very high-priced attorney, whatever his reputation, may feel that you're simply a small fish and don't rate his best effort. Let's take a very rough figure of $150/hour, and a typical uncontested divorce, with no special problems regarding the property settlement. A total cost of five hundred to one thousand dollars is in the ball park. A difficult case, with disputes over division of property, alimony, and child custody, can easily run you five thousand dollars, or more.

Fees vary from one part of the country to another, as well as between individual attorneys. The time to inform yourself is at the outset, before jumping in with both feet. The local bar association may be able to offer some figures. Better is the sum of the experiences of several friends. They may be able to guide you regarding which attorneys in your area are competent to handle divorces, and their fees.

Start calculating what your attorney will cost you. Begin with an optimistic low number of hours for a simple divorce:

HOURLY FEE x NUMBER OF HOURS = LOW TOTAL

_____ x _____ = _____

Now let's triple the number of hours, to allow for special problems that will consume more of his time:

HOURLY FEE x NUMBER OF HOURS = HIGH TOTAL

_____ x _____ = _____

If it gets really nasty, and legal proceedings are prolonged, it may total even more. Another factor that can affect what attorneys (note the plural) will cost you is whether or not, in your state, it's customary for the husband to pay for both attorneys. Find this out before you begin, but remember that it's negotiable in an out-of-court settlement.

Lost Earnings

Let's calculate the effects on your earnings. As with the attorney's fee, it's pretty simple. You need to list your hourly wage, and add up the number of hours lost from work. When calculating the times, remember the less obvious costs, such as:

- Contacting a moving company
- Filing a change of address
- Arranging for electric service
- Arranging for a telephone
- Arranging for water service
- Arranging for garbage pick-up
- Arranging for cable service
- Changing your driver's license
- Changing your car insurance

Will you be able to do any of these from work? In some states, a new driver's license is required, and this involves a personal appearance at the motor vehicle bureau. Your insurance agent can arrange changing coverage by phone, but he probably keeps regular office hours. If you can contact him at home, during the evening, this will help you. You'll have to contact your utilities during regular business hours, though.

Some attorneys keep evening or Saturday hours. This can save you time lost from work.

You'll also have to spend time and postage notifying friends, relatives, magazines, and others of your address change. You can do this during your off-hours, but stationery and postage will cost you a few dollars.

Court hearings always take place during business hours, except for a few cities where night court takes care of arrests during that time. Divorces, however, always take place during daytime hours. Court time is very variable. You may luck out, and get your case heard at the appointed time, or not, depending on the efficiency of the courts in your locale. Some judges are conscientious, and treat the people who appear before them as if their time is as valuable as their own. Others don't care, or are lazy, or simply inept. This sort can keep you cooling your heels for hours.

If you look very carefully at all possible ways you can lose time from work, you'll be discouraged. Use the figures, however, to help you plan so that you lose the least time from work. If you work nights or week-ends, you can take time during business hours, standing only to lose a little sleep. If not, you may be able to swap shifts with someone who works nights in your company.

Consulting attorney	hrs.
Apartment hunting	hrs.
Moving	hrs.
Court or deposition time	hrs.
Total	hrs. x Hourly earnings =
Grand Total: $	

Moving Expenses

What will the moving company charge you? Often, you can obtain an estimate from their sales representative. The basic formula is the hourly charge multiplied by the number of hours they estimate it will take to carry out the move, adding any extra charges to the total. Extra charges can be for packing, boxes needed to pack your goods, loan of wardrobes for moving clothing, and any special handling charges for special equipment.

Also include the charges for transfer of utility services. You may have to pay a "transfer fee" or a one-time "start-up fee." This is because a service technician has to come to your new address to turn on the power, or gas, and to check that the meter is working properly. You may have to put down a deposit if you use a new utility. There should be no charge for telephone transfer, however. You can find out about these well in advance:

Moving estimate _____

Telephone transfer _____

Electricity start-up _____

Gas start-up _____

Water _____

Garbage pick-up _____

Cable start-up _____

Also included in moving expenses are the costs of setting up in your new home. For example, buying a basic stock of food, only enough for a few days, can easily cost you a hundred dollars. Other household items add up to more. You may need to buy some second-hand furniture just to have a place to eat, or sleep. A good vacuum cleaner can cost you a hundred dollars. Make an estimate:

Food stock   _____

New appliances   _____

Furniture   _____

TOTAL: $ _____

You may be pleasantly surprised by your friends, some of whom may eagerly lend or give you some items and appliances they no longer need. Some may offer to lend or give you old furniture, a vacuum cleaner, or even a TV set. Others may try to ease the transition by inviting you to dinner one or more times.

Property Split

If you live in a community property state, assets and debts are split 50/50, in principle. From the worksheet in the financial section, take your net worth and divide it in half. This is what you may lose right at the outset.

Long-range Costs

We've already noted that certain types of income, such as royalties and residuals, can be very vulnerable because your wife can lay claim to half on the basis that you earned them while married to her. If you own patents, copyrights, or have other such income, and haven't cashed them in, payments can stretch for years, with your wife taking half each year. You can calculate what this might add up to over the years, and your lawyer can help you calculate "present-day value," because settling for a lump sum today is in your interest. You may have to give up your interest in the house you jointly own to get her off your back, but it's worth it, especially if you expect your royalty or residual income to rise during the next few years. If you expect it to drop, but can fool her lawyer into thinking it will rise, you can booby-trap the agreement. However, if she's got any sort of handle on you, such as alimony or child support, her lawyer can seek to have these increased to compensate. This is why a clean break is preferable.

We've already discussed the motives of certain women in trying to obtain alimony and child support payments. They know that such payments can be financially crippling, and greatly diminish the ex-husband's dating desirability or prospects of remarrying. There have been enough such cases to make this a real danger.

It could happen to you. If you're breaking up a marriage which produced several children, and have a wife who, for one reason or another, cannot work, you're likely to be stuck with their support. The judge won't care about your wife's hidden agenda. He'll only be concerned with the dollars-and-cents of support for her and for the kids. He'll sock it to you, even if it means lowering your lifestyle almost to the poverty level.

Let's add up these costs:

Alimony, per month	. . . .
Child support, per month	. . . .
TOTAL	$ . . . .

Let's take a shot at calculating what this will cost you in the long run. First, list each child, and multiply his or her support payment by the number of months until the eighteenth birthday, the usual cut-off date for support payments:

NAME   PAYMENT   x   MONTHS   =   TOTAL

_____

_____

_____

_____

_____

_____

TOTAL FOR CHILD SUPPORT: $

Now list your wife, and your estimate of how long you'll be paying her alimony. If in doubt, because you can't reasonably estimate her prospects of re-marrying, or how long she'll live, add the months until you reach age 65, retirement age.

PAYMENT   x   MONTHS   =   TOTAL

$

Now let's try for a grand total:

Children   _____

Wife   _____

GRAND TOTAL $ ____

If you retain custody of the children, you'll have to calculate your costs differently, because you may have to, depending on their ages, arrange for a day care center. These can be expensive, and you'd better find out the cost in your area before you make your move.

The good news is that your ex-wife won't have it as easy as she may anticipate. If she thinks that she'll continue in the style of gracious living to which she's become accustomed, she's wrong, unless you're terribly wealthy. The hard fact is that the pie gets split more than two ways. The lawyers get theirs first, and what's left goes for moving and living expenses for both of you. Each person's share is definitely going to be significantly less than 50% of the total assets.

You also have to count the costs of living apart. How much does it cost you to maintain a separate household? Work out a monthly budget, keeping in mind that you have to calculate the costs for yourself and for anyone living with you, such as children.

Now compare this with your monthly income. Keep in mind that you may have to make temporary or permanent support payments to your wife.

Household Budget

Item	Monthly	Quarterly	Yearly
Rent or Mortgage			
Homeowner's Insurance			
Real Estate Taxes			
Electricity			
Natural Gas			
Water/Sewer			
Garbage			
Telephone			
Cable TV			
Home Maintenance			
Auto Loan			
Auto Insurance			
Gasoline			
Auto Repairs			
Health Insurance			
Doctor Bills			
Dentist Bills			
Prescriptions			
Groceries			
Household Items			
Laundry			
Clothing			
Entertainment			
Gifts			
Other:			
TOTALS:			

Emotional Costs

These can be devastating. People have committed suicide during and after divorces. Keeping yourself on an emotional even keel is a major goal in your efforts to survive divorce.

Some people are more vulnerable than others. You may truly be the strong type who can get through it with few scars, either because you've been through it before and have become battle-hardened, or because you have inner strength. You also may need emotional support during and after divorce. This is where a friend or girlfriend helps.

A major error, unless you're in really bad shape, is to see a psychiatrist. If you need counseling, a better choice would be your clergyman, if you're religious. If you're a member of a support group, such as Alcoholics Anonymous, there are many other members who will be able to help you.

Another major error is to try to cope with your loneliness by joining a dating club, or dating service. Some are outright scams. Even the honest ones are poor prospects, because people who need dating services tend to be the losers who can't find friends on their own. A letter to Ann Landers, published on February 20, 1990, summed it up well. The author was a woman, but men have had comparable experiences. Membership cost $699 per year, and benefits included receiving several names of eligible male members each month. She met six men through this service, including one who was grossly fat, a married man, one who came to a date without enough money to pay for a cup of coffee, a heavy smoker with emphysema, another who took out his false teeth during dinner, and an ex-con who had served time for rape.

Another poor way to meet women is in a pick-up bar. You may find a good one, but the odds are overwhelmingly against it. If you think otherwise, ask everyone you know where he met his wife. How many met their wives in bars?

A bar-fly is likely to be alcoholic, or otherwise undesirable. Bars also attract eccentric types, such as professional teases, who promise a lot and deliver nothing. It doesn't take long to spot a tease, unless you're so desperate that you lose your objectivity, but you can waste time and money with a tease, and it can ruin an evening.

A Last Word

Look before you leap. Make sure you know what you're doing before you take any action. This is especially true if you're contemplating marriage, because a bad marriage can be very costly.

You've seen how the law, and current court practices, favor the woman. Keep this in mind if your marriage is starting to slip, and plan carefully to minimize your losses. Make preparation as early as you can, to reduce the stress and work-load you'll face if your relationship collapses. Don't tolerate a bad situation because you either don't know what to do, or aren't prepared to take corrective steps.

Most importantly, seize the initiative, and retain it. If, through good-natured tolerance, you let a bad situation ride, you're losing. You must play to win. If you don't, she will.

13

Getting Help

There are several organizations devoted to the rights of separated and divorced men, and the issues involved in child custody. Several have also disappeared, and it's important to verify the names and addresses with an authoritative source, such as the *Encyclopedia of Associations,* before expending time and postage.

America's Society of Separated and Divorced Men
(ASDM)
575 Keep Street
Elgin, IL 60102
(312) 695-2200
Richard Templeton, President

This organization is strongly pro-male, with a viewpoint that many lawyers handle divorces poorly, mainly for their own benefit. The organization provides individualized counseling regarding legal rights, and refers members to local attorneys known for their pro-male stances.

Membership dues are sixty dollars for out-of-state members, and eighty for Illinois applicants. Membership is a pre-requisite for individualized case-work. Applicants fill out an application form and a four-page case work sheet, which covers the details of each situation, including children, money matters, and legal issues.

> Fathers for Equal Rights
> PO Box 010847
> Flagler Station
> Miami, FL 33101
> (305) 895-6351
> Mr. Welch, Contact Person

This organization will send you a brochure describing their resources and services for a stamped, (75¢) self-addressed envelope. Fathers for Equal Rights sells an array of materials bearing on divorce, custody, and related topics, and you'll have to decide whether their helpfulness to you is worth the price.

Both organizations may also want you to accept collect telephone calls, and it's important to let them know in your first letter whether you're willing to do this or not. It's tactful to explain to them that there is no urgency, and that you are willing to wait for the mail to bring you the information they send. You may also explain that your funds are limited, and that you simply can't afford to pay for telephone calls.

YOU WILL ALSO WANT TO READ:

"Yes, there are books about the skills of apocalypse — spying, surveillance, fraud, wiretapping, smuggling, self-defense, lockpicking, gunmanship, eavesdropping, car chasing, civil warfare, surviving jail, and dropping out of sight. Apparently writing books is the way mercenaries bring in spare cash between wars. The books are useful, and it's good the information is freely available (and they definitely inspire interesting dreams), but their advice should be taken with a salt shaker or two and all your wits. A few of these volumes are truly scary. Loompanics is the best of the Libertarian suppliers who carry them. Though full of 'you'll-wish-you'd-read-these-when-it's-too-late' rhetoric, their catalog is genuinely informative."

—THE NEXT WHOLE EARTH CATALOG

THE BEST BOOK CATALOG IN THE WORLD!!!

We offer hard-to-find books on the world's most unusual subjects. Here are a few of the topics covered IN DEPTH in our exciting catalog:

- *Hiding/concealment of physical objects! A complete section of the best books ever written on hiding things!*

- *Fake ID/Alternate Identities! The most comprehensive selection of books on this little-known subject ever offered for sale! You have to see it to believe it!*

- *Investigative/Undercover methods and techniques! Professional secrets known only to a few, now revealed to you to use! Actual police manuals on shadowing and surveillance!*

- *And much, much more, including Locks and Locksmithing, Self-Defense, Intelligence Increase, Life Extension, Money-Making Opportunities, and more!*

Our book catalog is 8½ x 11, packed with over 750 of the most controversial and unusual books ever printed! You can order every book listed! Periodic supplements to keep you posted on the LATEST titles available!!! Our catalog is free with the order of any book on the previous page — or is $5.00 if ordered by itself.

Our book catalog is truly THE BEST BOOK CATALOG IN THE WORLD! Order yours today — you will be very pleased, we know.

LOOMPANICS UNLIMITED
PO BOX 1197
PORT TOWNSEND, WA 98368
USA